HORSE SENSE
For the Leader Within

EXPANDED EDITION
An Equine Guided Approach to Self Leadership

Ariana Strozzi

This book is dedicated to my children,
Paloma, Wesley and Jack
And my grandson, Chance,
Who inspire me beyond words

A new voice is coming forward
as loud as the day
and the night together
Calling a distant, yet familiar sound
and as the call comes nearer
I recognize the voice saying

"Come here, come close"
And in the stillness of a breath
a new world comes to light
as if inspired by some
darkness of night that not even a
firefly feels a need to light.

Ariana Strozzi

TABLE OF CONTENTS

ACKNOWLEDGMENTS

I owe the gift of my heart to my first horse, Sumi, who really set the wheel in motion that ultimately inspired this book. Her unconditional love and swift beauty galvanized a lifelong pursuit of harmony and connection with the natural world. She was my first teacher of commitment, perseverance and forgiveness. She gave me a place to belong when I felt alone and patiently waited for me to arrive at each new path on our journey together.

Thanks to Lacey and all of the horses, hawks, owls, eagles, bobcats, coyotes, rabbits, ravens, sheep, goats, dogs, cats, snakes, lizards and turtles in my life who have held up a mirror to my soul. Thank you for the great mother earth, the sky, the ocean and the wind and storms for humbling me to be exactly who I am supposed to be.

I wish to thank my mother for her love of animals and intuitive nature and my father for his scientific mind and artist's heart. I thank the great-grandmother I never knew because it was her passion for the natural world that has compelled me to follow my path even when I did not know where I was going.

This book would not be possible without the love and support of my children, Wesley, Paloma and Jack who are my ground and inspiration, my grandson, Chance, who is full of joy and passion and my man, Rick, who is my rock. I would also like to thank Jessica Murray for guiding me back to myself at just the right time.

And finally I would like to thank my students at SkyHorse Ranch and all of the other places they have graced my path for their commitment to learning and growing and for plowing the field through which I have become a teacher.

INTRODUCTION

A naked man on a naked horse is a fine spectacle;
I had no idea how well the two animals
Suited each other.
— *Charles Darwin*

It was a beautiful spring morning on the rolling hills of coastal California when I first recognized the parallels between the principles of horsemanship and human leadership. Though I initially rejected the idea, thinking that it was just my imagination, something caught my attention. When I looked again, I became fascinated with this new insight.

Was it possible that two very different discourses could be integrated into a revolutionary new way of developing the whole self? I started experimenting with this notion, watching it evolve day by day as I practiced and observed, experimented and risked letting go of what I knew for something I didn't know. And so began a journey into how horses could help us let go of old fears and encourage us to lead ourselves into the future of our design.

I had arrived at a game worth playing: a discourse rich in meaning and purpose. Leadership as *followership* comes to life as we learn to step outside of our human confines and reconnect to the natural world.

This book is about the profound applications of horses as healers and teachers. It explores and defines the foundational principles of Equine Guided Education and the 'horse as healer/teacher' process. Horses model the essential qualities of trust, authenticity, honesty, intuition, listening and a willingness of spirit. Horses have no agenda with us; they simply reflect our strength of character, our heart, our internal incongruence and our self-limiting perceptions. By example, they ask us to lead our lives with the same dignity, grace, and power that they naturally embody.

Horses help us close the gap between how we actually present ourselves to others distinct from how we *think* we are being. The minute our bodies get close to them, they size us up, asking, "Who is leading?" They expect us to embody what we care about and stay centered on the life we want to live. In so doing, they help us understand that leadership begins with the *self* we are.

The question, "Are you leading your life or is it leading you?" becomes the topic of exploration. By becoming aware of our animal nature and our innate drive for survival, we develop the capacity to *respond with choice* versus *react* to the pressures of life.

The following pages reveal that the underlying principles of horsemanship parallel the concepts associated with human development, growth and learning. Horses teach us how to find self-acceptance in a world of judgment. As we learn to think more like a horse, we develop our intuitive imagination and create new possibilities for our lives. Rather than focusing on what is wrong with us, we shift our attention towards what we are naturally good at. On this path of *becoming* we focus on staying connected to what has meaning and purpose.

As we develop a sensate awareness of our surroundings, and ourselves we find new ways to refine our authentic presence. We allow ourselves the privilege to think from a less linear perspective. We begin to trust that the nonverbal communicators of intuition, energy, intention and curiosity are resources to finding harmony within ourselves.

This book is divided into three sections. The first section, *Connecting to the Natural World*, is an introduction of sorts. It begins with an exploration of our fascination with animals and is followed by some notes on my personal journey of defining this work. The last chapter in this section defines nine principles of *Intuitive Leadership* that are universal to understanding humans and animals from a biological perspective.

4

The second section, *Are You Leading Your Life or Is It Leading You?* focuses on the first three principles of *Intuitive Leadership*. We begin this conversation with the notion that leadership is a fluid, changing process that defies absolute definition. *Leadership as followership* and *self-responsibility* become the topics of exploration.

The quest for self-responsibility requires evaluating our automatic assessments about leadership and exploring more flexible interpretations that allow us to find *choice*. In this process we reflect on how we respond to life before thought. We remember that we are born with a natural fear for survival, an innate desire to be social and to feel like we *belong*.

The third section, *The Nonverbal Language of Animals and Humans*, focuses on the other six qualities of *Intuitive Leadership*; the nonverbal, energetic qualities with which we communicate and coordinate. Research shows that ninety three percent of our communication is nonverbal. My hope is that by bringing our awareness to the nine principles discussed in this book we can collectively become more authentic, more honest and more accepting of ourselves and those around us.

I have chosen to use the gender term 'she' in discussing the principles of this book. My decision to do this was based on keeping things simple and trying something new. By no means do I mean to offend men or any other person. Many of my clients are men. Since many other publications historically have been written in the male gender, I felt it was a reasonable time and place to use the female gender in this book.

The case studies presented include real situations. I have changed the names of some of the individuals and some locations for confidentiality purposes. The horses' names are their true names. I am grateful for their profound contribution to this book.

PART ONE

CONNECTING TO THE NATURAL WORLD

THE ARCHETYPE OF THE HORSE

Although horses may be workhorses and farm horses
pulling their loads of civilization, dream horses still carry
heroes on their backs, both in the images of dreams and in
the invisible myths that accompany those images.
— *James Hillman*

Lacey isn't what you would think of as a typical leader. She does not own a phone, a computer, a calendar, a car or any of the normal things you would think that a leader should have. She does not live in a house, but rather a field. She stands on four legs and does not speak our language. And yet, she is a teacher of leaders, having spent years leading her own herd as well as thousands of humans who have come to the ranch to develop their leadership presence.

Lacey has an amazing ability to reflect each person's unique style within minutes, offering tremendous insights to her students. For some, she becomes a resentful employee, dragging her feet through every task asked of her. For others, she comes to life in graceful movement that inspires even the most skeptical. With amazing generosity of spirit, Lacey accepts each new person with fresh eyes and willing curiosity.

I have never met a person who is not awed by the swift, strong movement of an impassioned horse. Throughout history the horse has represented the archetypal virtues of honor, integrity, beauty, strength, loyalty, pride, durability and perseverance. Horses have a tremendous capacity to forgive and start anew. Their beauty and courage reflect these qualities in our own bodies and in our dreams of dignity. Horses are tame and yet wild at the same time. They reflect our individuality while still being part of a community.

The glorious image of the western cowboy or the Native American warrior and his trusted mount live on in our imaginations as a rare bond of mutual respect and partnership. In more modern times our imaginations have been fascinated with the horse/human bond in stories such as *The Black Stallion, Black Beauty, Spirit* and *Seabiscuit.*

The Black Stallion told of a rare bond between a spirited racehorse and a young boy, while *Black Beauty* reflected the good and bad relations that a horse experiences with humans. The animated movie *Spirit,* is about a wild horse who, while untamable, encounters both the worst and the best in men. While he goes through entrapment and frustration, his spirit remains free and becomes and inspiration for any wounded spirit longing to be free.

Seabiscuit, a national best-selling book and hit movie, reveals how an average racehorse, whom many simply gave up on, became not only famous in the horse racing world, but became an icon for the "little guy" who makes it big. Hildebrand tells the story of how a horse nobody else wanted inspired and healed three broken men to be more than they ever thought possible.

Seabiscuit surpassed idol status as a famous racehorse during the World War II era. He was a mascot of hope and possibility, power and endurance during a time of depression and poverty. He was an average looking horse with crooked knees, but his spirit and determination lifted the hearts of millions of people.

Over seventy thousand people would travel for days despite hard times to watch him run a two-minute race. He was so important to the American spirit during the depression that in 1938 Seabiscuit was on the cover of more newspapers and magazines than Franklin D. Roosevelt and Hitler. Seabiscuit is a simple reflection of how important the horse has been to the human psyche, especially in hard times.

THE ART OF HORSEMANSHIP

The ancient art of horsemanship has been traced back to at least 8000 B.C. Horses were easily domesticated because of their social nature and inquisitive spirit. Through a process of mutual adaptation, their utility grew to include transportation, labor, military power, companionship and sport. The Celts, Greeks, Indo-Europeans, Iberians, Berbers, Persians, Bedouins and Asians revered horses as companions of the gods having special healing powers and, in some cases, as gods themselves. In the Roman Empire, horses were emblems of wealth and power, as only the wealthiest of men could enter chariot races. Many rulers collected horses as displays of their wealth and stature. One emperor of China had over 400 horses buried with him when he died.

In fact, there was a registry for equine aristocracy before there was one for human beings. John Jeremiah Sullivan writes in his *Harper's* magazine article:

> *Theognis, a Greek poet of the sixth century B.C. wrote to a friend that in "horses…we seek the thoroughbred, and a man is concerned therein to get him offspring of good stock; yet in marriage a good man thinketh not twice of wedding the bad daughter of a bad sire if the father give him many possessions."*
>
> *(October 2002, pg. 55)*

Whole cultures and ways of life were built around horses. Many historians believe that horses inspired the industrial revolution, since they made it possible to travel great distances. Once we became accustomed to this new mode of transportation, we wanted to get there faster, inspiring the invention of the automobile. In the early 1900's, motorized engines, rated by their *horsepower*, began replacing horses. It's hard to remember that the first automobiles were looked down on because they were smelly, created dust and noise, unlike the horse-drawn carriage.

Some of us have grown distant from our horse partners, but less than a hundred years ago whole cultures of people including

Americans relied on horses in some way or another. In fact, in the early 1900's there were more farriers than there were physicians. Horses enabled the farmer and rancher to work faster and more effectively. They tilled fields, removed tree trunks, carried produce to market and doctors to the sick.

In some third world countries such as Afghanistan, the horse is still heavily relied on for transportation, physical labor and warfare. Even in America the horse is still an integral part of a few ranching operations because horses can go into terrain where vehicles cannot. Today horses are valued members of police units and search and rescue teams for the same reasons. But over all, their utilitarian usefulness has dramatically dwindled.

Even at the turn of the twentieth century people were still around horses everyday whether they were using horses for farming, transportation or warfare. Even people walking down city streets were surrounded by horses moving about, whinnying, and negotiating with each other at the tying posts. I believe that this regular habit of being around horses required a broader sensory awareness or *common sense*. We often call this having a 360-degree view.

Imagine in less than one hundred years how much we have become desensitized by our machinery, electricity, noise and air pollution. Some people don't go outside for days, let alone get sensory stimulation from the natural world through trees, plants and animals. Walking down a city street filled with horses is lost upon our current practice of walking down a city street filled with honking cars, unhappy people and a bombardment of metallic noise.

WARFARE

The basic spirit of the horse to be part of a team was a major factor in the effective use of the horse in the cavalry and military. Perhaps this is where the concept of *management* developed, since the successful coordination of a team of men and horses requires training and practice. In actuality, the word, *manage* means "to train or direct a horse", while the word, "leader" means "one horse placed in front of the others".

Twenty-four centuries ago, Xenephon wrote about how the training of one's horse centered on creating a team that moved as one, where clear communication was invisible and the team's actions were fluid and concise. Great pride was taken in the *Art of Horsemanship*.

The great Lipizzaner stallions are perhaps the finest modern exemplars of the warrior's trusted steed. They were trained to jump up and kick the enemy and their cannons in battle. The modern discipline of dressage was an integral training program for the cavalries of both Britain and the U.S.

A warrior's steed was often as famous as his mount. Robert E. Lee's horse, Traveller, was so revered that when he died he was buried next to his master. That means that someone took care of Traveller after Lee's death and very purposefully assured his resting place next to his man. It was an honor to be the individual who cared for Traveller's grave and was imbued a lifetime of dignity.

"The battle for freedom was won on the back of a horse." This quote tells not only a historical reality, but also gives light to our deep connection to the horse. This was our reality less than five generations ago. Today we have to strain our minds to have even a mild appreciation for the gravity of this statement. Yet the sense that horses offer us *freedom* continues to inspire us.

Many stories of equine bravery go untold or are lost in old books, but one story lives on of a little mare of unusual intelligence who was part of a troop of U.S. Marines in Korea during the Korean War. The sorrel mare, named Reckless, became an invaluable member of the Marine platoon. Her job was to carry heavy shells for the recoilless rifle and other military equipment over rugged ground. She would often make trips alone between the ammunition supply point and the gun site, laden with heavy shells under the most devastating enemy fire. She could string more communication wire in a day than ten marines.

The troops became very attached to Reckless and she would often sleep in the Platoon Sergeant's tent. She was even known to eat potato chips and drink coca cola with the men. She was a boost to morale and a well of compassion during the strain of heavy combat.

The troops would never have been able to succeed in their mission without this little mare. She was so instrumental during her war efforts that she was promoted to the rank of Staff Sergeant and a framed picture of her still hangs on the walls of U.S. Army Hall of Fame.

When she returned home to Camp Pendleton to retire in green pastures, orders were given that nothing would ever be placed on her back other than her blankets. The following is a quote by Corporal Jesse Winters:

> *"I remember asking how I was to exercise her if I could not get on her; that's when I learned that I was to run alongside until she got tired and wanted to go back to the stall. Lucky for me she knew the word oats and I could usually get her to cut her runs short.*
>
> *I remember that when she retired as a Staff Sergeant, I was not permitted to lead her in the parade because she out-ranked me and I could not give her orders, so they found a ranking NCO for that duty."*

As recently as 2001, a team of U.S. Special Forces responded on horseback to a warfare situation in Afghanistan. The horses were the only effective mode of transportation into the rough back-country as quoted from *Face the Nation*, November 18, 2001

> *Paul Wolfowitz (Deputy Secretary of Defense): If you would indulge me for a minute, I have with me a dispatch that came from one of our Special Forces guys who is literally riding horseback with a sword with one of the Northern Alliances.*
> *Bob Schieffer (CBS News anchor) With a sword?*
> *Wolfowitz: With a sword, with the Northern Alliance group of several*

hundred people who had nothing but horses and rifles. And he said, "I'm advising a man…how best to employ light infantry and horse cavalry in the attack against Taliban tanks, mortars, artillery and machine guns," a tactic which I think became outdated with the invention of the Gatling Gun…It's in a sense, the return of the horse cavalry, you might say, but no horse cavalry in history before this could call in air strikes from long-range bombers.

Schieffer: Do these people—do the people in the Special Forces know how to ride horses? I mean, there is a difference in jumping on a horse and hanging on and being able to ride. Are they trained to ride horses?

Wolfowitz: I can't say for sure, but apparently these guys were. They're trained in an extraordinary range of survival skills and quite an amazing group.

RECREATION

As the automobile and other machines replaced the horse, the art of horsemanship lives on in a variety of disciplines. In 1997 the horse industry was recorded as a $25.3 billion industry—roughly as large as the apparel manufacturing industry and the motion picture industry combined. If you take into account spending by industry suppliers and employees, the industry has a $112.1 billion impact on the U.S. economy. As of 1998, there were 6.9 million horses in the United States.

These statistics are a statement about our continued need to have horses in our lives for emotional and spiritual reasons even though they are no longer necessary to our physical survival. Riding horses is known to be good for the soul, a kind of meditation, a relief from the pressures of the world. Their honesty of communication captures many. We long for their reflection of us, accurate and untainted.

Any horsewoman quickly learns that she cannot muscle the horse into task, but must find a subtle process of communication that establishes a relationship of respect. She discovers that the horse listens, not to her agenda, her tools, or her words, but to her inner story, her inner commitment to what she cares about. Over time the horsewoman realizes that the relationship she has with her horse often mirrors the feelings and emotions she experiences in her personal or professional life.

Today, the recreational use of horses can be as simple as a good trail ride where the dilemmas of the world disappear into a rejuvenation of spirit. Or it can be a field for developing strength of character and empowering personal extension into the world. In addition horses become healers of wounded spirits, re-connecting the lost souls to the natural world and ultimately to themselves.

GIRLS AND HORSES

Over seventy percent of girls go through a phase in which they daydream incessantly about horses. Theory has it that the horse represents the beauty and power that they desire, right at the time the pressures of their sex and age squelches their self-confidence. A girl can live her self-confidence on the back of a horse in a way she is unable to do in her everyday life. The beauty that the horse reveals on the outside is the same beauty she longs for on the inside. The horse is strong and powerful and her ability to ride the horse proves that she too can be strong and powerful. Thus horse-crazy girls who actually get to ride horses on a regular basis cultivate a relationship with power that can inform the entire arc of their lives. Many of these horse girls go on to become high level executives.

I have found that over seventy percent of the most powerful executive women I have met or worked with rode horses as teenagers. Over thirty percent of them continue to ride in spite of their busy career lives. I believe it is because they learned from the horse how to be assertive, confident, declarative and passionate and they translated these qualities into other areas of their lives naturally and without thought. Most don't relate their present leadership abilities to their earlier years of practicing horsemanship. They take for granted that moving a thousand pounds of living mass is not as easy as it looks on the surface, and neither is human leadership.

As a young girl I became addicted to how easily my complicated world fell away when I was at the barn. The world was reduced to the horses and me: our spirits becoming one, the wind in our hair, the open landscape, breath and movement, breath and stillness. The horses saying to me with every step, "Are you with me?" Calling me to be present and mindful.

When my relations with humans were confusing, I found safe harbor with horses. They didn't care if I made a mistake or had a bad hair day. They always offered their spirit wholeheartedly and asked me to be as beautiful as they, as powerful as they. I would stretch myself beyond what I thought I could possibly do just to show them I could. And so, in those early days of my life, horses were my first teachers of the fundamental principles behind all leadership: believe in yourself, commit yourself to what you believe in, and assert yourself wholeheartedly.

When I wasn't at the stables, my friends and I would play "horse" for hours taking turns being horses that had *good owners* and horses that had *bad owners*. The *good owner* symbolized a person you looked up to, admired and wanted to serve or do things for. The *bad owner* was demanding and unfeeling, forcing his leadership upon us, and we followed him with a broken spirit because we had no choice—not dissimilar to the good boss, bad boss phenomenon or the antiquated command and control method of leadership.

Without knowing it I was already learning how to relate to my human life from an equine perspective. I was learning a new way to lead myself and relate to others from a relationship perspective rather than a dominant subordinate process. I could have easily missed the opportunity to transfer my relationship skills with horses to the human world. But at specific juncture in my life I had no choice but to see humans from a horse perspective in order to understand them and accept them.

EQUINE GUIDED EDUCATION

As our industrial dependence on horses has significantly dwindled, the 'Horse as Healer' has dramatically increased. It is as if we inherently know that we need them to rekindle our psycho-spiritual vitality. We are re-*membering* that they connect us to the natural world, to compassion, to love and to honesty. We are witnessing the transformation of the modern horse as these powerful animals become teachers, healers, coaches, mentors, mediators, and body workers. The emergence of programs that involve horses as emotional and spiritual guides has increased by over three hundred percent between 2001 and 2003 and as 2010 has reached a common level of public awareness.

This relatively new application of horse sense is rapidly expanding into a wide variety of educational and therapeutic modalities. Workshops on *horses and negotiation skills, horses and self-esteem, discovering self through horses, horses and parenting, horses and coaching* are gaining popularity. Special programs are being crafted to develop relational skills for policemen, martial artists, war veterans, youth at risk, and medical students. Each month, new offers of horses as guides and teachers spring into form.

The Equine Guided Educator creates a supportive environment for clients to learn about themselves and develop skills relevant to the life they say they are committed to creating. The horse "guides" the exploration of the client's inner world and how it relates to their external ambitions or stuck places. The word *guide* meaning "someone who can find paths through unexplored or unknown territory."

The human facilitator translates into words the horse's kinesthetic insights and feedback about the client's mental, physical, spiritual, emotional and social well-being. Through the process of evaluating the client's current patterns of behavior, perceptions of possibility (or not), and habits of responding to life, the Equine Guided Educator encourages the client towards a healthy self-image and supports the exploration of new practices for achieving personal or professional goals.

The combination of the human educator (coach, therapist) and the equine guide offers unique, powerful, experiential exercises geared towards developing self-knowledge and self-responsibility. Some common topics of exploration include:

o   Identify old stories and habits that are no longer effective
o   Refining one's ambitions and goals for the future
o   Enhancing communication and relationship skills
o   Encouraging self-confidence and self-esteem
o   Developing trust and respect for self and others

Experiential sessions with horses have been proven to circumvent the interruptions in healing and growth that our psychology often suffers. The desire to connect with an animal that cannot speak our language eloquently closes the gap between self-image and social perception. In the latter chapters of this book we will explore this subject further.

Many people feel safer with animals than they do with other humans. Animals can bypass underlying trust issues that complicate relationships between humans. Horses and other animals are honest reflections of themselves *and of us* at each moment. The experience of finding our alignment of mind/body/spirit in unison with an animal's mind/body/spirit gives us faith and a reference point for finding the same empathy for our fellow humans.

The client's willingness to trust the horse and accept its feedback occurs in minutes, as opposed to the weeks or months that it can take with a human coach or therapist. The client sees the horse's feedback as genuinely constructive and embraces it with a deep desire to become a better human for the horse's sake.

People from all walks of life and cultural backgrounds intuitively understand that a horse has no agenda with them. Horses have an amazing ability to reflect the inner workings of the human, moment by moment, and relate differently to us in each new situation. Horses accept, in some grand way, all the great aspects of us and, at the same time, the most embarrassing, shameful aspects. They do not judge us or make us *wrong*. They do not cull us from the herd or exclude us, they wait for us to find our authentic expression, no matter how unique, and befriend us when we tell the truth. Their patience, their openness to see us in a new light each moment and each day, and lack of judgment is a pivotal concept that humans could study for a lifetime: A concept that reveals compassion, empathy, relationship and acceptance of self and others.

As seen in the 2000 movie *28 Days*, rehabilitation facilities take their patients to a ranch to work with horses on rebuilding their sense of self worth. This part of the movie models existing programs for people in rehabilitation, youths at risk and prison inmates. These programs have found that incorporating *Horse Sense* into the self-development process helps people regain self-esteem and a sense of self-responsibility. Participants can rebuild trust easily with the horse, which may seem impossible for them to do with other people. The movie, *The Horse Whisperer*, further opened the door to the horse as healer phenomenon.

Handicapped riding programs provide handicapped individuals with a place to bond, build trust, have social contact, develop muscular strength and coordination, and physical exercise. The rhythm of the horse's walk approximates the motion of our walk. A person with physical disabilities can develop atrophied or damaged muscles through the reflexive motion of horseback riding. Numerous reports abound of people with MS and other diseases can relearn how to walk again after spending years in a wheel chair. There are even seeing-eye horses for the blind and handicapped. These miniature horses live longer than dogs, see greater distances and can carry heavier loads. They have been successfully house trained as well.

Perhaps our relationship to horses is interwoven in our genetic makeup and we are reinventing how we connect to their wisdom and the opportunity they provide to balance our inner life with our external reality.

IT'S ABOUT A *"WAY OF BEING"*

Descartes said, "I think, therefore I am." That 'I am'
has never seemed to me worth ruminating about. Of
greater consequence is 'who' I am.
—*Susan Chernak McElroy*

Some of my best teachers have been horses. Growing up with these honest beings provided a natural training ground to learn patience, resilience, confidence, and perseverance. My first horse, Sumi, mentored me through the trials and tribulations of adolescence. Sometimes she was my mother, sometimes a bossy sister, but most of the time she was my best friend. I knew she loved me, but she certainly didn't let me get away with anything. She constantly challenged my ideas and insisted that I believe in the possibility that I could change. When I was unconfident and unclear, she was a thousand pounds of immovable flesh. When I was engaged, present and giving clear directions, she was beautiful, powerful—even mystical. Her beauty and willingness to love me inspired me to figure out how to be better *for her.*

The other horses I took care of at the various stables of my youth were each their own mirror of relationship. Each one had a different personality and a different idea of how they expected to be treated. Being less than five feet tall at the time, I learned early that getting the horse to go along with *my* ideas was not about muscular strength or wishful thinking. I had to ask the horse to follow my lead by *some other means.* What I learned about leadership in those early days eluded reasonable explanation until I began to teach people how to ride and train their horses.

Whether I was cleaning stalls, grooming and exercising horses, or caring for their injuries, there was a constant negotiation about who was in charge. The more innocent and resilient I was, the more easily the relationship developed. The more I knew—the more agenda I asserted—the more complex the relationship became.

I was fortunate in those early days to work with horses that lived in herds where I could observe them engaged in their hierarchal politics on a daily basis. Their degrees of negotiation ranged from subtle cues to exaggerated displays of assertiveness. Their actions were direct and to the point. They did not relish overpowering or humiliating other herd members. They enforced their assertive nature only enough to establish a clear line of communication. They did not abuse their ability to influence other herd members. They were not sentimental, and yet there was a fondness and caring for each other that inspired even my skeptical heart.

Humans, on the other hand, seemed far more complex. The gang of girls who hung out at the stables was a mirror of dominance versus submission. The more confident, pretty girls dominated and controlled the more passive, less confident girls. I guess the unconfident girls allowed this because they did not think they were either pretty enough, smart enough or athletic enough to stand up to the *cool* girls. It wasn't nice, but it was full of the social dynamics of finding one's place in the human herd. I often wondered why the younger girls put up with the abuse. More than once, I came to their defense, but most of the time I felt like an outsider looking in. I just wasn't interested in the fight.

I was often grateful that I was too busy doing ranch chores to get dragged into their politics. Quiet moments cleaning stalls or the walk up the far hill to catch horses were much more satisfying. Within a few summers most of the girls had sold their horses and left the barn to drive around with boys.

Over the years and many stables later, riding teachers also came and went. I seemed to be the only constant besides the horses, the fog and the windy weather. Most of the masterful horsewomen I encountered were not at the top of the page when it came to human social skills. What I mean is that they were socially awkward and had little time for social banter. In fact they really did not communicate well with words. They were like lead mares with either their ears pinned back, lost in thought or mildly interested in conversation.

Perhaps they had found the world of horses to be a safe reprieve from the confusing world of humans. They did what came naturally to them and didn't stop to ponder how to apply horse sense to their human students. They displayed many different styles of leadership from *command and control* to *inspire by presence*. I watched some horsemen dominate and subordinate their horses, while others quietly elicited top performance in a virtually invisible manner.

My first dressage teacher spent the first six months of my training yelling, "Use your seat! USE YOUR SEAT!" I would try this and I would try that, all the while wondering what the heck she was talking about. One day I felt a connection to the horse I had never felt before. The arduous practice of trying to learn what she meant was at the same time an invaluable training ground for me to experiment with new concepts. One day I changed the way I was breathing, and as she yelled once again, "Use your seat!" I took a deep breath and imagined I was dropping its weight deep into my saddle, and for the first time she responded, "That's right." She never told me to use my breath, but that discovery opened up a whole new world for me as a rider.

Under the pressure of competition, where I only had one chance to do it right, I learned the importance of concentration. Not mind concentration, but mind-less concentration: a focus on the goal without thinking or judging, assessing or questioning. It's the art of being fully present in the moment. One moment of thought-full agenda could turn the running river into a dry gully.

The sting of failure in full view of the various spectators of my life was a sufficient motivator to ride with full commitment and without thought, but an even stronger incentive was not wanting to let Sumi down. She was an amazing jumper. If I headed towards a jump with an internal question like *Will Sumi refuse the jump?* —She would. To succeed, I had to truly believe that we were going over the jump. It was not a question.

Sumi taught me early on not to waste her time or mine if I wasn't serious about making something spectacular happen. When I popped into my head and cockily thought we were going to win, we would make a silly mistake so trite I knew I had only myself to blame. When I wasn't thinking about winning, but just doing what we both loved to do, we would gracefully speed through the course faster than any other horse and rider team.

Over the years I trained at different ranches with their own unique rules and particular methods of training horses. At each ranch, there was an unspoken rule, "This is the way you work with horses, and if you don't do it *this way*, then you don't know anything about horses." I resisted this rule, as I found it controlling and lacking in imagination. Wanting to know everything about horses, I remained open to every methodology and so learned many different techniques and tools for training horses.

To this day, many modern horsemanship methods have this unspoken rule. It runs rampid in the horse world. Why? I don't know. I think often it is someone's way of trying to distinguish themselves. There is a difference in saying, "this is my way," as opposed to, "this is THE way" and therefore implies that how others is doing it is wrong. I don't think that is necessary.

I wondered why so many horse people were set in their ways of doing things. Their apparent rigidity seemed to reduce their ability to learn new things and even to work effectively with some horses. In the horse world I grew up in there was a lack of openness to other points of view or sharing knowledge with other horsemen.

This one-way prejudice just didn't work for me. I began to ponder whether the methods I had already learned elsewhere weren't just as effective as the new methods I was being introduced to. I began to prefer some methods to others, because they were consistently more effective. I also noticed that some horses learned better with English techniques and tools while others learned better with Western.

So, naturally I began to observe what the more respected riders were doing that worked consistently with different horses. I became less interested in their tools and techniques and more interested in *who they were being* when they were directing the horse. I watched their mood, their tone of voice, their mannerisms, their body language. I wondered, *What is it about their presence that the horse listens to and respects?* I even noted how I felt watching them and the horse. I listened as I imagined a horse would listen. Did I (the horse) feel relaxed, tense, interested, or bored? Was I (the horse) happy, scared, dull, or sparky?

I noted that master horsemen and horsewomen, whether they were dominating or encouraging towards horses, were consistent and reliable in their actions. The horse knew they were sure about what they were asking for. Whether through fear and intimidation or invitation, the master horsemen were clear and focused. They weren't asking the horse a question, "Would you like to go into a trot?" They were saying, "We are going to trot now." This unspoken confidence often disappeared when they left the arena, but when they were with horses there was no question about their sense of purpose.

I also saw that while all these masters could get the horse to do what they wanted when they wanted, the horse was not always a full participant. To have a horse move around correctly, but with an attitude that was resigned or depressed, didn't inspire me. On the other hand, an impassioned horse that loves his work and is inspired by his rider captures my attention. I realized that I didn't want to just move a horse around by subordination. I wanted to engage the horse in a win-win game.

The qualities of inspired presence became clearer: when the trainer was authentic and her thoughts matched her outer expression, she embodied her goals and the horse could rely on her cues. The clarity of her intention energized a certain quality of movement in the horse. Her confidence helped the horse feel direction and purpose. Listening with an intuitive awareness allowed her to lead by listening rather than by dominating.

I also observed that bringing an openness and curiosity to the relationship allowed the trainer to include the horse as an equal partner and embrace the horse's point of view. These qualities generated a soft strength, a quiet resolve. I realized that, contrary to popular opinion, *there really are very few rules to training horses.* If I remained curious and open, I could find a way to reach each horse's spirit and desire to be part of a working team.

In my early years of teaching horsemanship, I noticed that when the rider was ineffective, the horse would become increasingly frustrated. I felt the tension between horse and rider, and struggled to help the pair resolve their conflict. I would instruct the rider on the proper use of her legs and hands. This had limited success. If the rider was tentative and fearful, the horse would become afraid and agitated and how she applied her hands and legs seemed to be a moot point. If the rider was distracted and not paying attention, it seemed unreasonable to ask the horse to perform in the absence of emotional commitment. Sometimes I would get on the horse myself and reflect on what I was actually doing in an attempt to discover some other way to work with the situation. Through this I slowly began to find words for the qualities of energy and presence that I had been observing.

It became apparent that the more emphasis the equestrian placed on her tools and techniques, the more the horse became a tool in her agenda about successful horsemanship, and the further away the horse's heart and spirit wandered. Without the horse's heart, we may have performance, we may have the horse move through a series of exercises that look magical to the uneducated eye, but do we experience the resonance, oneness and partnership that horses have with each other?

When we fell in love with horses, did we fall in love with making the horse do a series of tricks? Or did we fall in love with the possibility of becoming like the horse and all the horse represents in its archetypal presence?

26

CONNECTING TO THE NATURAL WORLD

Animals seem to belong to a family from which only
humans are estranged.
— *Thomas McGuane*

During my studies of animal social systems at U.C. Davis in the early 1980s, my native beliefs about the natural world came to the foreground with a deep resonance and practicality. It was then that I first realized that my native view was all but forgotten to most of the people I met walking down the street. In fact it was often looked down upon. At least I had found an arena where I could explore my ideas without complete judgment from others. Foremost among this forgotten reality was the knowledge that *we are our biology*. We are animals driven by the same biological drives as our animal relations. Feeling, sensing the world with our somatic senses, our animal body responding to the environment around us like a fine tuned dousing rod.

I began to understand how our industrial civilization and technological era has distanced us from our animal relations and thus from our own sensate wisdom, our first and primary information gatherer. Instead we rely on our mental acuity to interpret and rationalize our circumstance. Regardless of our rationalizations, our animal body and sensate awareness continues to respond first before thought or reason; our consciousness composed of more than our intellectual reason and mental abilities.

Our mental acumen can only provide us with partial answers about how we make sense of the world. The animal body responds first and foremost to the energetic changes in our immediate and perhaps even distant environment. The mind is limited to creating interpretations about our bodily experience. These interpretations can be either healthy or unhealthy stories that forward or hinder our ability to move into our life with clear focus and choice.

It's in this nanosecond between bodily experience and mental interpretation that trouble can start. It is here where we are taught not to believe our body and to rely only on our mental acuity, and thus are conditioned to become uniquely *human*. We are told that our intuitive, animal responses are wrong because if they were right, things might get a little uncomfortable periodically because we would be telling *the truth*.

Schools are set up to classify people rather than seeing them as unique individuals. Better to dumb us down, strip us of feeling. It's easier to control us this way. Once stripped of our own sensate wisdom, we can be properly conditioned to behave 'appropriately'. To learn more about how our schooling system strips us of our senses, take a look at John Gatto's book, *A Different Kind of Teacher*. Following is a brief paragraph of his discussions:

> *"Schools train individuals to respond as a mass. Boys and girls are drilled in being bored, frightened, envious, emotionally needy, generally incomplete. A successful mass production economy requires such a clientele. Whereas, small business and small farm economies, like the Amish, require individual competence, thoughtfulness, compassion and universal participation. Our own economy requires a managed mass of leveled, spiritless, anxious, family-less, friendless, godless, and obedient people who believe the difference between Coke and Pepsi is a subject worth arguing about...*
>
> *What schools are about in their structural design is dependency, obedience, regulation, and the subordination that an orderly system needs. Schools achieve these goals by endless exercises in subordination...Schools make childhood surreal by the application of Kafka-like rituals: They enforce sensory deprivation on classes of children held in featureless, sometimes windowless room: They sort children into rigid categories by the fantastic measure like age-grading and standardized test scores: They train children to drop whatever they*

are occupied with and to move as a body from room to room at the sound of a bell: They keep children under constant surveillance, depriving them of private time and space: They forbid children their own discoveries, pretending to posses some vital secret which children must surrender their active learning time to acquire.

Herbert Spencer, the great British philosopher and publicist on Darwinism, wrote a remarkable book entitled Education in the early 1860's in which he pronounced government schooling a preposterous endeavor doomed to failure. He said that this would happen because it deprived children of raw experience and responsibility precisely at the moment their natural development demanded it...in 1895 the president of Harvard said this: "Ordinary schooling, by confining children to books and withdrawing their attention from visual objects, renders the senses useless. It produces dumbness."

We are coming into a time where it is imperative to re-learn how to listen to and respect our sensate, intuitive animalness. Yet, in order to get to know more about our natural selves requires a humbling of sorts, an acknowledgment of our place on the same plain upon which all animal species live and die. We are part of a larger whole, a web of life, each species linked intrinsically together in a grand cosmos that scientific reason cannot quite explain. Nor does it need to. We don't need science to prove that all is interconnected. This basic instinct lives inside each one of us.

When this instinct, this ancient knowing, is broken by societal pressures and lack of outdoor experience in the natural world, our animal body becomes wounded. Our spirit self becomes disconnected; lost from its roots.

Some individuals resort to denying their bodily sensations, relying on mental acumen alone to get through life. This often works until their mid-forties or early fifties when the spirit self finally screams in pain and forces the individual to slow down or stop by creating actual physical dis-ease. The highly sensate, intuitive types (made wrong for their sensitivity) may also become dis-eased, but usually it is a mental disparity rather than a physical disparity. They begin to doubt or distrust the mental interpretations of their sensate responses. Native shamans recognize these forms of dis-ease in the individual merely as a symptom of the dis-ease in the whole (also known as the greater cosmos or circle of life), which includes the local surroundings comprised not just of the village people, but the neighboring trees, plants, rocks, birds and wildlife.

David Abram in his book the *Spell of the Sensuous* defines the shaman's role in healing and offers insight into the interconnectedness of all things:

> *"The traditional shaman acts as an intermediary between the human community and the larger ecological field, ensuring that there is proper nourishment, not just from the landscape to the human inhabitants, but from the human community back to the local earth. By his/her rituals, he/she ensures that the relation between human society and the larger society of beings is balanced and reciprocal, and that the village never takes more from the living land than it returns to it—not just materially but with prayers and praise. The scale of the harvest or size of the hunt are always negotiated between the tribal community and natural world that it inhabits...*
>
> *It is only as a result of her continual engagement with the animate powers that dwell beyond the human community that the traditional magician is able to alleviate many of the individual illnesses that arise within the community...hence the traditional magician or medicine person functions primarily as the intermediary between human and nonhuman worlds and only secondarily as a healer. Without a continually adjusted awareness of the relative balance or imbalance between the human group and its nonhuman environ, along with the skills necessary to modulate that primary relation, any "healer" is worthless--indeed, not a healer at all. The medicine person's primary allegiance, then, is not to the human community, but to the earthly web of relations in which that community is embedded.*
>
> *The most sophisticated definition of "magic" that now circulates through the American counterculture is "the ability or power to alter*

one's consciousness at will." In tribal cultures, that which we call "Magic" takes its meaning from the fact that humans, in an indigenous and oral context, experience their own consciousness as simply one form of awareness among many others. The traditional magician cultivates an ability to shift out of his or her common state of consciousness precisely in order to make contact with the other organic forms of sensitivity and awareness with which human existence is entwined. Only by temporarily shedding the accepted perceptual logic of his culture can the sorcerer hope to enter into the relation with other species on their own terms; only be altering the common organization of his senses will he be able to enter into a rapport with the multiple nonhuman sensibilities that animate the local landscape. It is this, we might say, that defines a shaman: the ability to readily slip out of the perceptual boundaries that demarcate his or her particular cultural boundaries reinforced by social customs and the common speech or language—in order to make contact with and learn from the other powers in the land.

Magic, then, in its most primordial sense, is the experience of existing in a world made up of multiple intelligences, the intuition that every form one perceives—from the swallow swooping overhead to the grasshopper on a blade of grass, and indeed the blade of grass itself— is an experiencing form, and entity with its own sensations and predilections."

The subject of our spirit and its connection to the whole is an important subject matter too detailed to discuss here. Suffice it to say our ability to contribute, to be part of the whole, becomes fractured when we are not connected to the greater cosmos in a spiritual sense. One of the greatest leaders of the 20th century, Martin Luther King envisioned this in his quote:

"In a real sense all life is interrelated. All men are caught in an inescapable network of mutuality, tied in a single garment of destiny. Whatever affects one directly affects all indirectly...I can never be what I ought to be until you are what you ought to be, and you can

never be what you ought to be until I am what I ought to be. This is
the interrelated structure of reality."

Native cultures around the world are based on the native
reality that everything is related. Deloria and Wildcat in the book,
Power and Place, which compares Native American metaphysics and
Western science say:

> *"The best description of Indian metaphysics was the realization that*
> *the world, and all its possible experiences, constituted a social reality,*
> *a fabric of life in which everything had the possibility of intimate*
> *knowing relationships because, ultimately, everything was related. This*
> *world was a unified world, a far cry from the disjointed sterile and*
> *emotionless world painted by Western Science...*
>
> *The Indian world can be said to consist of two basic experiential*
> *dimensions that, taken together, provided a sufficient means of making*
> *sense of the world. These two concepts were place and power, the latter*
> *perhaps better defined as spiritual power or life force. Familiarity with*
> *the personality of objects and entities of the natural world enabled*
> *Indians to discern immediately where each living being had its proper*
> *place and what kinds of experiences that place allowed, encouraged,*
> *and suggested...*
>
> *Today, as Western science edges ever closer to acknowledging the*
> *intangible, spiritual quality of matter and the intelligence of animals,*
> *the Indian view appears increasingly more sophisticated."*

Yet, many philosophers insist that we are separate from
animals and the rest of the natural world because we have
language. They rationalize that because we can coordinate and
plan into the future that we are smarter than animals. Our oral
language skills do not prove that we are not animals with biological
instincts. These philosophers forget that just because we do not
understand how animals communicate and coordinate, doesn't
mean they don't.

Elephants have a sophisticated communication system we are

only now beginning to understand. When an elephant dies, its herd members come back to the body two years later to scatter the bones. They may go off in different directions, but they plan their return ahead of time. Katy Payne of Cornell University has shown that these dynamic herd animals communicate via infrasonic sound waves and families can split up for weeks and meet again in the same time and place. They can communicate with these sounds that are inaudible to humans up to two and half miles away during the day and up to twenty-five miles at night.

Another researcher by the name of Caitlin O'Connell-Rodwell is studying how elephants communicate through the ground, not just the air using a form of seismic communication. Temple Grandin discusses in her book, *Animals in Translation*,

"*Theoretically we could have extreme perceptions the way animals do if we figured out how to use the sensory processing cells of our brains the way animals do…another reason for thinking everyone has the potential for extreme perception is the fact that animals have extreme perception, and people have animal brains. People use their animal brains all day long, but the difference is that people aren't conscious of what's in them.*"

Migratory birds, whales and dolphins also provide examples of sophisticated abilities to navigate into the future. Horses can sense the winter weather patterns ahead of time and grow a winter coat to acclimate to its forecast.

Who's to say who is smarter then? While our rational skills in conjunction with our language skills have created amazing innovations, it is these very innovations that are now threatening not only our ability to survive as a species, but also the earth as a living organism. Are we really so smart after all? Perhaps we are dumber than we think. I guess only time will tell.

Regardless of our opinions on intelligence, our attempt to distance ourselves from our animal relations not only detracts from *who* we really are; it sets up a dangerous separation from the natural world. The more separated we become--the more numb to sensation--the more soulless we become. The more soulless we become the more robotic and lifeless we become. Despair, depression and resignation become the predominant moods of our culture. We lose the will to fight for our freedom. We no longer know what freedom really means. We are truly lost.

"The paradox of our time in history is that we have taller buildings but shorter tempers, wider freeways, but narrower viewpoints. We spend more, but have less; we buy more, but enjoy less. We have bigger houses and smaller families, more conveniences, but less time. We have more degrees but less sense, more knowledge but less common sense, more judgment, more medicine but less wellness.

We drink too much, smoke too much, spend too recklessly, laugh too little, drive too fast, get too angry, stay up too late, get up too tired, read too little, watch TV too much, and pray too seldom. We have multiplied our possessions, but reduced our values. We talk too much, love too seldom, and hate too often...

These are the times of fast foods and slow digestion, big men and small character, steep profits and shallow relationships. These are the days of two incomes but more divorce, fancier houses, but broken homes. These are days of quick trips, disposable diapers, throwaway morality, one night stands, overweight bodies, and pills that do everything from cheer, to quiet, to kill. It is a time when there is much in the showroom window and nothing in the stockroom."
-George Carlin

When one looks at the vastness of the animal kingdom, it is impossible to assert that we humans are somehow dramatically different than other highly evolved animals except that we live out of balance. The assumption that our form of communication is somehow better or more sophisticated does not make any rational or reasonable sense in the big picture of reality. To acknowledge our place in the animal kingdom allows us the possibility of re-learning how to use our other senses, our *anima senses* waiting patiently to be recognized and encouraged. These sources of natural wisdom can lead us out of hopelessness and into courageous action. Our psychic, intuitive senses are mysterious and magical. They can connect us to the past and the future. They can travel on silent waves across the world. They have the power to heal, to accept, and even to imagine the healing of ourselves and the whole.

It is in this new reality that horses and other animals become our teachers, encouraging us to develop our sensations to trust our ancient knowing abilities. They teach us that truly *being in the moment* allows one to live gracefully with the Unknown. We do not need scientific justification or research to prove that the power of our imagination and the nonverbal skill of our will can change our trajectory. We do not need to wait for proof that the magic and mystery of the natural world contains all of the information we need to heal our planet and ourselves.

Perhaps horses have been selected by the cosmos and her other creations to be the messengers because we so readily identify with them. They are an undeniable visual reflection of us, the environment and the living senses in their wholeness. We easily identify with their archetypal virtues of strength, beauty, power, courage, wildness, and dignity. Perhaps we have more compassion, and therefore more willingness to listen, to the horse than a dragonfly or red-legged frog.

If we focus on what we have in common with horses and other animals, we see that many of the factors that influence other vertebrate species also influence our precognitive approach to life. We may be unaware of how our biology dictates our fears, ambitions, choices and decisions. Our biological underpinnings are further concealed by long-standing cultural and psychological beliefs that we can reason our way through life by intellect alone. However, many of us learn by trial and error that we cannot simply change our behavior and actions by making a decision to change. Our body holds all of our history, our memories and experience. We can tell our mind to think new thoughts, but we also need to connect those thoughts to our body's experience and to our spiritual underpinnings.

The majority of people who I work with are successful by any cultural standard. They have the right car, a nice house, and a great job title, but they are in a crisis of meaning. They often cannot understand *what is wrong* with their life. Yet their intuitive self knows that their mind/body/spirit is out of alignment. Their spirit self has become disconnected from the whole.

In order to create sustainable change in how we respond to the complexities of our lives we need to understand our biological predisposition to be in relationship to the larger whole. Many of us are so busy with modern technology, career advancement and the quick consumer fix we have forgotten our need to be part of the natural world. As our busy lives spiral us away from the natural world, the subconscious wisdom of our biological makeup calls us back. Our increased fascination with animal biology, native cultures, shamanism and altered states of consciousness provides pathways for us to reconnect to the natural world.

This desire to reconnect explains the dramatic increase in the equine and pet industry over the last several years. We are finding new ways to bring animals into our lives. In the past many of our relationships with animals were based on how the animal could be used for human benefit, like canaries in mines, horses and sled dogs for transportation, barn cats for rodent control. Now people keep animals because they want to have an intimate relationship with another living being. Dogs, cats, horses and birds are becoming our children.

In 1999, $20.9 billion dollars was spent on pets (not including horses). Over 60 percent of all American households have at least one dog or cat. The average American household spends more money on pet food than it does on wine, over-the-counter drugs, candy or television sets. We spend more money on veterinary services than on coffee, books, video rentals or computer software. My 86-year-old neighbor, who relied on his horses to plow the fields and drive him to town, would have a cow if I told him that people are now brushing their horses' teeth and house-training them.

What is this increased need for interspecies connection telling us? Is it confirming that we have become so disconnected from our own natural social systems of tribes and communities that we are reaching for any animal contact? Have we so damaged trust within our own kind that we are resorting to other species for intimacy and contact? Or have we innately realized that our mechanical and intellectual prowess that created the Information Age is spiraling us away from our instinctive need to be connected to the natural world?

This need to be part of a greater whole beyond our own species is one reason why we are incorporating the wisdom of the horse back into our lives. Horses still know who they are and operate with complete integrity of their inner emotions and spirit. As honest reflectors of our own animal ways they can teach us how to listen to our inner drives, desires, and fears. They insist that we respond authentically to ourselves and to others.

This quote by Dominique Barbier, from his book *Sketches of the Equestrian Art,* illustrates some of the virtues gained by staying connected to the natural world:

> *"Horses teach us how to ask without aggression, how to love without condition, and how to avoid the destructive side of perfection. They teach us to sublimate oneself through sharing, giving and healing. They teach us to cherish every single moment for its novelty and wonder and remain true to the best traditions of the past."*

But why horses? Why not zebras, deer or raccoons? Why do horses offer such unique opportunities for learning about authenticity, trust, compassion, and intuition? Is it the predator-prey dynamic as many people suggest, or is it more about our social, hierarchal similarities?

Since 2001, I have seen a dramatic increase in the reasons why people are attending my Leadership & Horse™ programs, which I have been doing since 1989. People would come to the program with statements like, *"I am not sure why I am here, but I am feeling called by horses."* Some people went on to say they weren't sure they even liked horses, but they were dreaming about them and thus the horse became a call toward something unknown that they couldn't help but to follow. So I began studying this *call*. If indeed people are being called, what are they being called to?

In asking this question for the last several years, my current theory is that the horses are a visible messenger or guide back towards the natural world. While butterflies, snakes, birds, dragonflies and other animals are also guides of nature, many people just don't notice them or their significance. A horse is undeniably visible and also taps into our ancient recognition of archetypal virtues.

Horses are calling people from all over the world and all disciplines to re-awaken, to learn to listen to their animal body. In this re-awakening and learning how to use our anima senses we can re-connect to the Mother Earth and all of her creations. We can learn how to find our own freedom and in so doing let others free as well. We can learn to create sustainable practices for living in which man and animal can live and flourish in a natural balance with the land and sky.

Exploring what we have in common with horses as opposed to our differences allows a whole new world to open up. That being said, I would like to demystify the overrated and inaccurate statement that it is the horses' prey nature that allows our relationship with them to be possible. I think when we overemphasize this aspect we miss this new world entirely and remain in an outdated concept of relationship and correlation.

PREDATOR/PREY DYNAMICS

Many of today's modern horse professionals are saying that the dynamic tension between our differences, the horse as a prey animal and the human as a predator, explains why our relationships with horses work. They explain that it is the horses' prey nature that has the horse fear us. Yet, having worked with many predator and prey species in my zoology career, I would have to say that any wild animal fears us in a similar way. If you put a coyote or mountain lion in a round pen or a confined it to a stall it would resort to very similar behaviors that we commonly see in the horse.

In addition, these equine professionals are misinformed and misusing a specific term common in the science of biology. The zoological definition of *prey* is an animal that is killed and eaten by another species. The definition of *predator* is an animal that preys, destroys or devours another. The predator is a carnivorous animal whose entire muscular skeletal system is designed to hunt and kill its prey. The prey animal can be either be a herbivorous or carnivorous species that is found commonly in the local environment of the predator species.

Predation is a way of life in which food is chiefly obtained by killing animals. The relationship between a predator and its prey forms an intricate strategy that contributes to ecosystem equilibrium. In wild populations, predation plays an important role in maintaining the population size of prey animals and since predators tend to only take the weak, old or sick, it helps to assure strong, healthy populations of prey species. The coyote and the rabbit are a good example in that the coyote's role as predator is fundamentally important to managing the population of the rabbit.

The predator-prey relationship is complex and important, but it does not explain our relationship to the horse. As human beings, we may become *predatorial* when we attempt to manage the control of a species by killing and eating it. We would have to have an intertwined history of killing horses and eating them in order for a horse to consider us its predator. In the field of biology, we are not considered a predator; we are an omnivorous animal who can also be preyed upon.

The wild horse, and particularly the domestic horse, does not see us as a lion threatening its survival by trying to eat it for dinner. Instead the horse senses our intention to separate it from its herd, capture it and domesticate it. Yes, the horse is afraid but his prey nature does not explain his fear. Perhaps he wants to flee simply because his instinctive fear is that he will be isolated (*a terrifying notion to a horse because of its social nature*), and that we will aggress upon him and dominate our will over him forcing him to acquiesce his free spirit and natural ways.

Even a herd of horses can feel when the human is consumed by his/her desire to control and manipulate his/her environment. The horse sees this as being completely out of integrity with the natural *way of things*. The more the human imposes his/her will upon the horse, the more he/she tries to dominate the situation, the more out of integrity with *the whole* he/she becomes. And thus the horse is driven into a deep instinctive fear for survival. In this state, the horse can be completely engulfed by his fear. His fear for survival can become so predominant that the horse can actually fall into a psycho-spiritual death, in which the horse either loses his will to live or his spirit becomes lost and he literally goes crazy loco, and consequently unmanageable.

Some wild horses have been killed by humans in an effort to manage their populations, but the ancient bond between man and horse far supersedes these occasional atrocities. The horse in ancient times would often follow the human tribe from location to location, drawn together rather than apart. Domestic horses when born in captivity do not see the human as a predator, but as another herd member. Let's remember that as humans we are omnivorous animals, historically combining several strategies of hunting and gathering to survive. The raccoon is also an omnivorous animal, and we do not consider the raccoon to be a predator. So why are we assuming that we are predators to the horse? The horse is strictly herbivorous, a natural prey animal for carnivorous predators, but so are gazelles, zebras and deer. Why then have we been unsuccessful in domesticating these other prey animals? Why is our relationship with the horse so unique?

Our successful domestication of and subsequent relationship to horses cannot be rationalized by its prey nature. So rather than focus on a predator-prey relationship that does not exist between man and horse perhaps it is better to ask, "How does the horse's sensate, somatic nature impact our relationship with them?" "How are we similar in the way we see the world?"

Perhaps the domestic horse isn't afraid that we are going to eat him, he is afraid that we will exile him, that we will not accept him into the herd, or that we are being intensely inauthentic and cannot be trusted. When we approach the horse as if to dominate it and impose our will upon it, it may resist such subordination, for inside it still knows it is free. Isn't that free will in a horse, their sense of freedom part of what we fall in love with? What we may be interpreting as *prey* response to our loud gestures and dominating tactics is really a startled response questioning our lack of connection. I have seen many a horse, gentle with one person and completely terrified of another. I am sure if you have had any significant time around horses you have too. And you know in your heart it is not because the horse is a prey animal and we are the predator. So let's end this silly discussion.

Assuming that we do not want to engage in a predator-prey relationship with the horse, what other factors allow a natural substrate for communication to be present? What do horses and humans have *in common* as opposed to our differences that allow us the potential to truly unite and blend our core energies together to create something larger than either individual alone could manifest? If we look deeper and more fundamentally at our commonalities we find that horses and humans have a pre-verbal understanding of each other driven by similar social, hierarchal strategies for survival.

Of the 4,250 mammalian species, we have only successfully domesticated fourteen of them, and only five are important on a global scale: the horse, the pig, the sheep, the cow and the goat. Jared Diamond, in *Guns, Germs, and Steel*, writes in detail on this subject. His studies on the domestication of animals clarify the unique virtues that allow us to develop long-term bonds with horses.

One significant factor is their reasonable disposition. Out of the eight species of wild horses and their relatives, only two have been domesticated: the horse and the North African ass. Despite numerous attempts to domesticate the other six, they are too aggressive and antagonistic towards humans, whereas horses are curious and willing to give us a chance. Another factor is that horses are less nervous than other herbivorous prey such as deer and antelope. Deer panic and scatter when threatened. Horses on the other hand, bunch together following the direction of the lead mare and will sometimes stand their ground when threatened.

Diamond goes on to note that the majority of domesticated large mammals have three similar social characteristics: they live in herds; they maintain an ordered hierarchy among herd members; and different herds occupy overlapping home ranges, rather than exclusive territories.

ANIMAL SOCIAL SYSTEMS

In the vast animal kingdom there are only a handful of animal social systems that repeat with slight variations and spin offs. Horses, dogs, cats and many bird species form social, hierarchal bonds. In fact their social systems are similar enough to our own that a natural substrate exists explaining the ease with which these animals have become so integral in our lives.

Animal societies are made of individuals who belong to the same species and live together in a cooperative manner. A society is distinct from an aggregation of individuals because the individuals rely on other members of the group in order to increase chances for survival. Each member of the group contributes to the collective survivability of the whole. Living in social groups requires a process of communication. The more socially interdependent each individual is to other members, the more a process of coordination is also required. In insect societies, communication is primarily an exchange of chemical stimuli, whereas in primate societies, relationships are personal and based on recognizing members of the group as individuals.

Most social animals understand their interdependence on others. Humans, on the other hand, seem burdened with ambiguity. Perhaps it is because we have rationalized that we are separate from the animal world that we complicate our basic social drive with the rebellious notion that we could just be an aggregation of individuals doing our own thing. We now have disposable friends, lovers and marriages. It is so easy now to just disengage and move somewhere else.

Animals seem to be much more in sync with the fact that they belong to a social order that is deeply integrated and intertwined in a complex system of relationships with other species and the natural world as a whole. In addition, they know they cannot just move away from their social community, or get online and make new friends.

David Abram's words excerpted from his book *The Spell Of the Sensuous,* summarizes our historic efforts to distance ourselves from the natural world:

> *"According to the central current of the Western philosophical tradition, from its source in ancient Athens up until the present moment, human beings alone are possessed of an incorporeal intellect, a 'rational soul' or mind which, by virtue of its affinity with an eternal or divine dimension outside the bodily world, sets us radically apart from, or above, all other forms of life....*
>
> *In Descartes' hands, two thousand years later, this hierarchical continuum of living forms was polarized into a thorough dichotomy between mechanical, unthinking matter (including all minerals, plants, and animals, as well as the human body) and pure, thinking mind (the exclusive province of humans and God). Since humans alone are a mixture of extended matter and thinking mind, we alone are able to feel and to experience our body's mechanical sensations. Meanwhile, all other organisms, consisting solely of extended matter, are in truth nothing more than automations, incapable of actual experience, unable to feel pleasure or suffer pain. Hence, we humans need have no*

scruples about manipulating, exploiting, or experimenting upon other animals in any manner we see fit.

    Curiously, such arguments for human specialness have regularly been utilized by human groups to justify the exploitation not just of other organisms, but of other humans as well (other nations, other races, or simply the other sex). Such justifications...locate 'humans' by virtue of our incorporeal intellect, above and apart from all other 'merely corporeal' entities."

Focusing on our differences—the horse as prey, human as predator—supports our historic need to *dominate over* so that we can feel in control. By taking a different tact and focusing on our commonalities, we expand our range of relating to horses as sensate beings who can help us find our way back to our own nature and our own need to be connected.

A friend who is a retired pastor of a church told me a story that illustrates not only an individual's need to be socially connected, but also how easy it is to help others get reconnected to place and community when we stop seeing them as objects or inconveniences.

FRANCINE FINDS A HOME

Francine was a homeless woman who visited my friend's church to receive free meals and a place to sleep on cold nights. Most people walked by this scruffy woman on the street embarrassed as she talked to herself, the cracks in her path or the bushes in the park, but when she visited the church, she was greeted with a hug and a warm smile by the pastor. She would bring him photographs of the sidewalk and tell him long stories about what the lines in the pavement meant. My friend understood her need to connect with another person and to share her stories. He decided to give Francine a home and the task of preparing the dining hall for dinner. Over time, she took to her new responsibility with a quiet smile and dutiful hands.

At each meal, she greeted the visitors with the same kind heart with which the pastor had first greeted her. As she began to feel good about herself, she made new friends. Her dependability was quickly recognized by a local restaurant that took her in, gave her a bed in the back room and a job cleaning the restaurant.

Francine still visited church regularly because it was a family to her. One day, when the pastor greeted her, Francine pulled him aside. She thanked him for taking her in and she told him that she was happy now. She no longer heard voices and felt that she belonged to people that she could take care of.

The pastor's story touched my heart. I felt as if I knew this woman. She looked like a palomino filly, somewhat fragile, but big-hearted. She had become lost from her herd and from the essential sense of being part of the whole. Through the kind act of the pastor, she had reconnected to a herd that she could contribute to and receive a kind gesture or warm smile in return. She was at home once again.

Having a sense of belonging is vital to living a rich and meaningful life. Accepting the fact that we are a social, hierarchal animal allows us to gain insight into how we can navigate the concrete streets and silent allies. Knowing our place in the various hierarchies of our lives enables us to find the best situations in which to place ourselves.

SOMATICS AND SPIRIT

"Youth is not entirely a time of life—it is a state of mind. It
is a temper of the will, a quality of the imagination, a vigor
of the emotions, a freshness of the deep springs of life. It is
a predominance of courage over timidity, of appetite for
adventure over the love of ease.
—*General Douglas MacArthur*

The raven, sitting atop my prayer tree, talks to me. The horses in the field whisper words of wisdom. The wind nurtures my face with her gentle touch one day and the next whirls dust into my eyes so I cannot see. The earth holds me up when I am sad and wish to be invisible. She is always there for me, always waiting to catch my fall or enjoy my success. Sometimes she asks me to look at her beautiful spring poppies dancing in the wind. She tells me through the hawk's call that I already know the answer to my own question. I listen. I remember that I belong. Her sand feels soft and warm as I walk upon her. The taste of her berries makes me smile. It's hard to feel sad and lonely when I am with her.

The wounded child, who cuts herself so she can feel her pain (labeled in a mental institution with words I do not understand), sits on the ground as the black and white mare stands over her. The horse mother nurtures the girl. She was not asked to care. She just knows that this child needs her love and patience. The human mother knows this too, so she drives her the long hour and half to the ranch. She knows that no human can save her daughter, but a horse can.

The mother sits outside waiting, healing herself in the sun and the cool afternoon breeze without knowing. The girl tells the mare about getting behind in school, her friends doing drugs and pushing sex, her mother's disappointment with her. She loves her mother but she is not who her mother wants her to be. She does not want to disappoint her mother, but she has to be true to her own inner calling, one her mother doesn't understand.

She touches the horse's soft coat, and breathes the same breath. The breeze tickles her face. Her heart opens. She talks about the girl she draws on paper, over and over again, with dark lines under her eyes and tears running down her face. Her mother says that her drawings are morbid. But the horse thinks otherwise. And so a healing begins. The girl learns to be herself and to give her mother appropriate boundaries. Rather than cutting herself, she tells her mother that her comments are hurtful. And the mother learns to listen to her child, to see her with new eyes. This child of hers is an artist, one who walks lightly on the earth. She will not be an accountant, she will not live a "practical" life; it is not her destiny to do so. And so the mother, without knowing it, awakens to the wisdom of the earth. She no longer sees her daughter through human eyes. She finally recognizes and embraces her daughter's spirit. They drive the long road back to the city holding hands.

The somatics of the girl and the mother resonate with the somatics of the environment. Each is healed by the other. Where one begins and the other ends is inexplicable. The mysterious and magical healing of the horse and the girl, the mother and the sun, cannot be defined in textbooks or recorded on tape. And yet witnessing such beauty brings tears to one's eyes and warms a tired heart.

Somatics involves the pulsing, connected nature of all things, the sensate wisdom within all living beings: mind, body spirit in its wholeness. Perhaps the human's first angst begins with disconnecting from the great mother, the ultimate nurturer of the spirit. The notion that we can heal our hearts and find ourselves by just getting outside and listening, feeling, touching, smelling, tasting, is too easy. It doesn't require an education. It's scary to think that the years we have spent training our minds might be somewhat insignificant. It's just too easy to go outside and let nature do the healing.

Nature is not scientific; it needs no explanation, logical reasoning, or justification. She wasn't trained to justify her actions, to quantify her results. She is ever-present, all accepting, non-judgmental, patient, and resilient. Even though she is simultaneously merciless and non-sentimental, one knows that she is forever practical and wise. She is the pure embodiment of somatic sensibility. Definitions of Somatics include:

- *Somatics -- the art and science of the inter-relational process between awareness, biological function and environment, all three factors being understood as a synergistic whole: the mind, body, spirit as a unity. The unity of the self.*
- *Somatic -- of or relating to the body*
- *Soma -- "the experience of the body" as subjectively experienced by the consciousness that inhabits it.*

Some professions focus on the way the 'soma' itself responds to the environment; others focus on the way the mind interprets the 'soma's' response. What I am particularly interested in is the interconnectedness of the 'soma' to the greater cosmos: the unity of the mind/body/spirit and the energetic field (wherein the lack of unity with the living environ causes dis-ease).

The more we quest for the answer to *who am I*, the more we begin to realize that it isn't about 'I' at all, but rather, who I am in relation to *how I* contribute to the greater whole. When we recognize that our core self is inextricably entwined with the natural world, self-development becomes focused on *how am I destined to contribute to the whole of which I am fundamentally connected to.* By seeing the self as part of the whole, we transpose the symbolism of body/mind/spirit to self/other/world.

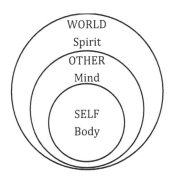

THE BODY

The body is the physical aspect (labeled as the *self* in the diagram) of our self as it relates to, contributes to, or takes away from the environment. The body holds all of the experiences and memories of our lives. It relates to the environment first. It is the part of the self that we need to listen to most -- the first informant -- the first interaction with change. In order to change our environment, we first have to change ourselves; the way our body interfaces with and responds to the environment. I like the saying by Barbara Rector, "I take full responsibility for myself and therefore contribute to the safety of the group." This implies that we cannot control others, but can only change ourselves, and by changing ourselves, we contribute to the potential change of our greater environment.

THE MIND

The mind is in the social domain of *other*. How we think about and relate to others, how others relate to us is the next immediate interface we have with the whole of the environment. We are social animals; our instinct is to care about how others perceive us. Often it is either our perception of how others see us, or how others tell us they perceive us that can produce either a healthy or an unhealthy self-perspective. For example, the story of the girl and her mother illustrates that the original dis-function arose out of mental interpretations by both the mother and daughter, and traveled out-ward to the daughter's interpretation of others including friends, teachers, etc.

Some ancient theories pose that to achieve mindfulness requires the detachment from the mind itself. Interestingly enough, the art and science of Astrology sees the *intellect* as only one of ten basic components of the human psyche. My favorite astrologer, Jessica Murray, writes:

"Humanistic astrologers see the mind as a tool of the life purpose, which itself is a tool of the soul. Far from being the seat of consciousness, the mind is merely an apparatus, a marvelous piece of equipment that serves or doesn't serve the whole person. There is quite

a gap between this view and the way most of us operate...It is a very old idea that in order to achieve excellence in any endeavor, from art and war to athletics, the mind must be disciplined into a concentrated state. The more practical of these traditions do not mention the lofty goal of enlightenment, but every one of them – from ancient martial-arts exercises to Silva Mind Control – proposes that our incessant internal yak-yak-yakking is an encumbrance to clarity and effectiveness."

THE SPIRIT

The spirit correlates with how the self orients with respect to the world, how the self connects to the environment and the larger cosmos of reality. This includes an individual's beliefs, ethics, and values. It includes the underlying destiny or life purpose of the individual. The mystery of past life experiences and the innate desire to contribute to the whole lives here. This seems to be the least studied area of somatics, perhaps because it is the most indefinable, the most mercurial and mysterious of the somatic domains. Historically reserved for witches, shamans, and quacks, this domain of somatics is the missing piece to current studies of dis-ease and what causes dis-ease. By re-connecting to her spiritual longing, this girl was able to re-interpret herself in relation to others in her life.

As mentioned in the previous chapter, in many indigenous cultures, the shaman or medicine person's primary function is not actually to heal the individual, but to heal the dis-harmony between the community of people and the natural environment within which the people live. I like the shift from disease (a focus on what is wrong with the individual's physical body or mind) to dis-ease, meaning more directly that the individual is not in ease or flow with its surrounding environment, which is made up not only of family, friends and the human community, but also the rocks, trees, wind, birds, and animals that surround the individual (or lack thereof). Transferring the focus from what is wrong with the individual (loaded with human judgments) to re-connecting to the original self (the spirit of the person) and the local environment allows an important shift in the individual's ability to develop a healthy self-image and more effective habits of relating to others and to the whole.

To access the spirit requires imagination and curiosity, a form of *not knowing and not requiring an answer*. As Henry Poincare, a colleague of Einstein wrote, *"It is by logic that we prove, but by intuition that we discover."* The native imagination begins in the realm of feeling and sensory awareness and emerges into consciousness through an ability to suspend certainty. It is in this precise way that horses can become our teachers, offering us a whole new world of sensory awareness where new insight and new interpretations can form.

Being in the presence of horses requires that we develop our other senses because the only way we can develop communication and partnership with them is through being present to somatic experience and listening to our intuitive sensations. When we are in our head, judging ourselves or doubting our intuition and somatic senses, we are literally not safe for the horse to relate to. When our mind, body and spirit are aligned (the energy flowing freely within and between), the horse becomes interested and willing to connect.

In team building and leadership development, the reliance on nonverbal communicators as the significant tools for developing relationships forces us into *practicing* leadership principles rather than *thinking about them*. In this way we train our willingness to let go of what *we know* for what we *don't know* and this becomes the ground from which we learn and develop new skill. In this more authentic state we develop a natural presence for leadership as opposed to a positional authority of control.

Aristotle spoke of 'ethos', as a type of leadership in which a leader influences others to change their values and thus their performance. He explained that ethos is not what a person says or promises, but it is their *way of being* in the world, their presence and comportment that affects others to follow them and be open to their ideas. A leader's success depends on her ability to lead a group of people creatively, effectively, and with exquisite vision through a variety of challenges and breakdowns. To do this well a leader needs to be able to listen with an open mind, communicate goals without emotional baggage, and assist each team member in finding a sense of purpose about their work.

Effective leaders understand that this type of leadership is a skill that is trained and developed, refined and nurtured. Michael Jordan, the famous basketball player said it well of his coach in his book, *For the Love Of the Game:*

> *"As a player you connected with the atmosphere the coach created. With Phil Jackson it was like we were in harmony with each other in the heat of the battle. We were comfortable not only with each other but also with the situation no matter how difficult the moment. We were able to find peace amid the noise, and that allowed us to figure out our options, divine solutions, and be clear-headed enough to execute them. That's what Phil brought to the Chicago Bulls and that's what we all connected with. That's one of the reasons we became so successful for so long. That presence, that peace of mind, that connection between the team and the coach was more valuable than anyone possibly could know. But that was Phil. That was who he was at the core of his being. It wasn't contrived. He taught us to find peace within ourselves and to accept the challenges; whatever they may be at whatever moment they appear. It wasn't just an intellectual passing out information. We were able to see the embodiment of those thoughts every day."*

SOMATICS AND SPIRIT

The body is the primary information gatherer, whether you are a human, dog, horse, or bird. The body responds to the environment first, the mind comes along after the fact and interprets the energetic stimuli present and makes an interpretation. At a biological level, the body responds with immediate speed, before thought, determining safety vs. danger.

Each person is a soma contributing to the energetic aliveness of the environment. Each animal and plant is also a contributing soma. Even the wind, the sun, the mist, the rain are contributing somas. And so begins the realization that each is influencing the other all the time, before thought, before cognition, before rationality. What can be gained by feeling the soma at its beginning, at its first and continuing interface with the environment? A stick can become a fairy wand or a weapon to defend the self. A shell can become a treasure, giving us strength and power.

Animals and nature teach us that our mental processes get in the way, literally clouding our ability to feel ourselves. We are the judgmental animal. Often it is our interpretations, (self-directed or felt from others), that begin to disconnect us from the world at large. We learn not to trust our feelings. Instead, we judge our feelings as wrong or invalid. When we reconnect to the land and animals, we re-member that our immediate environment, not our mental acuity, provides the answers and affirms our sensate feelings. By becoming part of our environment we have the opportunity to re-learn how to trust our 'feelings', our sensate responses. As a result we are better able to answer the primal questions like, "Do I feel safe?" "Am I scared?" "Do I feel connected?" "I am I doing what I am supposed to be doing with my life purpose?"

Nature reminds us, forces us, insists not only that we feel, but that we become aware of how we feel. That we need to trust how we feel. Sometimes the wind is soft and nurturing and other times it is scary. As we awaken to the deeper meaning of the inter-relatedness of all things, we are forced to realize how disconnected we have become. The feelings and sensations that arise from the earth can become overwhelming for some.

Perhaps some of the modern-day angst that many people are experiencing is really the angst of the earth herself. Perhaps the sadness we sometimes feel is really someone else's sadness traveling on the silent threads of the air around us. Perhaps the girl who cuts herself is truly connected to the pain of the whole. The hope is that she continues to re-source herself by being with animals and nature, to give her the emotional, spiritual and physical strength to let her own unique voice and expression grace all those around her.

INTUITIVE LEADERSHIP

The important thing is to be able (at any moment) to
sacrifice what we are for what we can become.
— *Charles Dubois*

Living close to nature and growing up within and among a rich world of animals, plants and magical creatures, I learned to communicate without words or thought. It seemed natural to communicate this way. My world made sense when I was around animals. During my time at U.C. Davis, I spent five years working with birds of prey at the U.C. Davis Raptor Center where we rehabilitated hawks, eagles and owls for release back into the wild. I also worked in the non-domestic ward of the UC Davis Veterinary Hospital where I handled zoo animals, snakes, birds, wildlife, and an array of reptiles. Horses remained an integral part of my life as I continued to work at a variety of horse ranches to support myself through school.

Through personal hands-on experiences the animals taught me the same lessons the horses had about presence, authenticity and trust, fear, belonging. Animals designed to tear flesh from bone, would look into my eyes and see me. I had the undeniable understanding that they could see deep into to me: my fears, my sureness, my underlying mood and attitude. I also got the distinct impression that if I was not completely authentic with my intention, if I had an ounce of pretense, they would not trust me. In fact, they might attack me.

Wounded animals knew I was there to help them and so did not fight and resist. We would converse in silence. Often, it was not until after our interaction that I would reflect on the profundity of our conversation.

After college I continued working at horse ranches, managing veterinary hospitals and volunteering at the Raptor Migration Center at Fort Mason, San Francisco.

In 1988 I met Richard Strozzi Heckler, who would one day become my husband, and began to study aikido and Somatics. Both of these pursuits involved people and realized I had grown rusty at human social interaction. Somewhere along the line I had lost my ability to make contact with humans on a superficial level. I was comfortable in personal one-to-one interactions, but socially, I was shy and distrusting of people. I was often confused by the disconnect between their words and their body language. I admired people like Richard, who were sociable and friendly.

I longed to feel safe with people, but in order to get there I knew that I had to change the way I perceived them. People came to our ranch every day for aikido, riding lessons, and to train in becoming better leaders. Every day I had to be social. As long as horses were part of the picture, I was grounded and relaxed; otherwise I felt like a social retard: awkward and unskilled. Since I wanted our visitors to feel welcome at our ranch, I knew it was up to me to learn a new way to be around them.

I remember one particularly hot day while riding my Arabian gelding, Cairo; I had an epiphany that would change my life. It wasn't an uncommon experience for me to have life changing revelations while on horseback. I was in one of those thoughtful moments, reviewing my present life and thinking about what authenticity really meant and why animals had so much of it while humans seemed to have so little.

I realized that if I didn't change my trajectory, I would end up as a happy hermit living on top of the hill with my animals, but I would continue to feel a big void with people. I also had a nagging feeling that I would fail to share a gift I had that could make the world a better place. I had no idea what this part meant; what gift I was destined to share. My intuition spoke loudly that I had some role to play in the human world.

At the time I did not fully understand why I didn't enjoy

people's company, I just knew I didn't trust many of them. I didn't feel comfortable feeling the disparity between their words and their energy. I didn't like the lies and the posturing: making one person wrong so the other could feel right. And I really did not like when their words did not match their actions.

I resisted the easy road and followed my intuition. I made a pact with myself to enter back into the world of people. At first I was afraid. I didn't know how to release the confusing energy that people carried with them, but then I realized I did not have to give up my animal ways in order to be with people. I could bring my animal ways into my relations with humans. I could be a stand for honesty and frankness. It wasn't an either/or world. I had found a new ground for self-study and a place to further my overarching inquiry about what the animals were trying to teach me. At that moment a red-tailed hawk flew overhead.

AIKIDO AND HORSEMANSHIP

Combining my horsemanship practices with aikido practices helped me to enter the world of people. I realized I had been studying the energetic elements of aikido with horses my whole life. The qualities of a person's chi or Energy, their groundedness or lack of it became more interesting as a way to identify why I was responding the way I was. I was well studied with this dimension with animals, but not with people. I learned that when I was distrusting and stiff with people that they too would have a rigid reaction to me.

I became more interested in how I could gain choice in how I responded to people as opposed to being at their whim. Being dyslexic, words and descriptions were often confusing to me. I was embarrassed and ashamed that I was not normal. I did not want anyone to know that I was not tracking in the linear way. In the study of aikido and somatics with humans, I learned how underground I had gone with my secret (my dyslexia) and afraid I was of being judged by others (which I often was). I learned to trust in my own senses of a person's energy and that that was more important than the words they spoke. I learned how to move beyond judgment, my own and others, and to find curiosity about what made people tick. I became curious about how and why people judged me, rather than defending against it. I developed my own ground, my own value system and allowed it to be ok that some people did not understand me.

How did I do this, you might ask? Well, I learned from the horses. I watched how they did not pass judgment on people, how patient they were at trying to understand the human once again. I studied their somatics and how they listened to their senses and to the energy of the person rather than the mind's idea.

As I compared what I was learning about communicating with people to what I knew about communicating with animals, I realized that the concepts of Somatics relate to the subtle, nonverbal cues to which we all unconsciously respond. These cues are pivotal to animal communication, and yet humans literally have to relearn how they respond to these unspoken cues. As human beings we have a unique ability to say one thing with our mouths and something completely different with our body.

Practicing and observing the martial art of aikido also influenced the way I shifted the lens through which I interpreted horsemanship. Aikido students practice developing a *center* (or base) from which they *extend* and *blend* their energy in relation to that of their opponent. Sally Swift's book *Centered Riding* is an excellent distillation of the principles of aikido into equine practice. Apparently Sally studied aikido with George Leonard, who was Richard's dojo partner for many years and with whom I briefly studied with and observed for many years.

One day, while riding Cairo, I realized that I was actually training in aikido principles while riding horses. I was practicing *center*. In horsemanship terms this might be considered *using your seat*. I was *blending* my energy with the horse's energy to create *one center*. In those golden moments when we were one unity, nothing else mattered. When I think of harmony, I think of those brilliant moments when the horse and rider become one. During these moments of oneness anything is possible.

I started thinking that it would be useful to bring aikido and somatic students out to work with the horses, because I had a sense that the horses could provide useful feedback in their practice of centering and extending. So began the opening of a whole new world of insight and discovery. When I incorporated the basic aikido principles of *centering, blending,* and *extending* into my horsemanship classes, I saw even people with no equine experience come away with valuable new insights into other areas of their lives. Beginner equestrians who started from these principles learned faster than seasoned equestrians who had to unlearn controlling habits.

Participants of my early clinics were shocked that I had somehow seen into their internal, private places. They wondered how I knew so much about them. "Are you psychic?" they would ask. Many would say, "I have the same issues at work!" or "This is what happens to me at home!" I realized that the horses were uniquely reflecting each person's patterns of thoughts, perceptions of reality, behavior and performance. The horses had a gift for revealing in the arena the issues that these students were facing in other areas of their lives.

It was somehow easier for the human to reflect upon these revelations in the arena because it wasn't another human giving them feedback. It was just a horse responding to them with interest, boredom, disinterest, frustration. The horse's responses were so unique and to the point, many participants experienced dramatic transformations in how they viewed themselves and others. By seeing themselves mirrored by a large, swift horse, they were able to quickly see new ways of dealing with the various situations in their lives.

Over the years I worked with people of all different shapes and sizes, responsibilities and experience. I began to see different leadership *styles* and levels of maturity in the leadership process. Over time, and through the horse's keen eye, I have come to appreciate that each different leadership style has its own validity; that one is neither better nor worse than another.

Most importantly, horses have taught me the virtue of

accepting each person's style, no matter how quirky or different. As long as a person is authentic, honest, and caring, they have the tools to find that resonance in life we all seek. Some leaders begin with great strength of character but lack follow-through, while others have a quiet endurance but not a lot of outward confidence. Other leaders can accomplish great feats by sheer will and force, but the cost is their health and well-being.

To squeeze a leader into a style that will never fit is both painful and fruitless. It is a far easier and more peaceful path to find the nature of the stream that each leader can thrive within.

I continue to this day (and over 5000 horse–human experiences later) to be awestruck and profoundly touched by the horse's keen ability to reflect each person's style, strengths and weaknesses. Horses reveal, without judgment, when a person is not disclosing emotional or psychological dilemmas. They sense when a person has lost her sense of meaning and purpose. They notice when a person is saying one thing on the outside, such as pretending to be confident, when on the inside the negative judge has a grip. They can literally see *inside* a person.

Their intuitive perceptions are so refined that they can sense internal conflicts, lack of confidence, doubt, and self-judgment in their human counterpart and reflect it back in a dramatic visual display of flesh and muscle. They can sense when an *old story* is stuck in the body and reflect it in cinematic clarity. They know when someone needs a good cry and magically encourage the tears to fall like wringing the water from a wet mop. They know when someone needs encouragement and when they need a good push.

The horse waits patiently for each of us to arrive at the core of our aspirations and to speak authentically from our heart. When we become authentic, the horse relaxes and becomes a willing and engaged team member. At the same time, the horse offers us yet another gift as a role model of compassion towards our fellow man.

Eventually I noticed that during sessions I was often feeling the same way that the horse was. As I practiced paying attention to my own response to each human I was working with, I was able to notice when I felt trusting, distrusting, bored, nervous, anxious, curious, loving. Watching the horse's response gave words to what I was feeling and reinforced my confidence in translating what I was seeing into human language.

I learned through experience that the energetic mirror that horses are for each participant directly correlates with other significant areas of their lives. I also learned that people accept feedback from a horse exponentially faster than they do from humans. People trust the horse's reflection as honest and direct.

I have found that for some mysterious reason, people are consistently motivated to change their behavior and performance *for the horse's sake,* much faster than they will change for themselves. Having someone else feeling the consequences of our actions gives rise to our desire to change, whereas our own psychological stories tend to spiral in circles ever inward, collapsing into a convoluted tangle of ineffective perceptions. The horse is an enlarged image of that *someone else.* People have a natural sense that they do not want the horse to lose. The desire to bring out the beauty and life of the horse inspires the human to step up to the plate of becoming responsible for his/her actions.

NINE PRINCIPLES OF INTUITIVE LEADERSHIP

I have attempted to condense the universal principles of both leadership and horsemanship into nine elements that comprise Intuitive Leadership. The following diagram summarizes each of the nine elements of Intuitive Leadership.

Bear in mind that while these elements are universal to communication, different methodologies may use different terminology in describing them. For example, the concept of confidence can also be considered courage. Some people refer to authenticity as integrity or congruence. Curiosity can also be considered flexibility or willingness. Subsequent chapters will deal with each of these concepts in more detail.

9 PRINCIPLES OF INTUITIVE LEADERSHIP	
BIOLOGICAL DRIVES (NATURE)	
Fear for survival	Knowing your fears Being able to take action in uncertainty
Social Instinct	Desire to be of value Knowing what you have to offer Being part of a whole
Hierarchy and Sense of Belonging	Knowing your unique gifts and where to contribute them
NONVERBAL COMMUNICATORS (NURTURE)	
Trust	Capacity to build trust
Authenticity	Inner thoughts match outer expression
Confidence	Centered on what you care about Taking a stand Lack of self-consciousness or doubt Having commitment and courage
Intention	Extending into the world with Energy Passion and desired intention 360-degree awareness
Intuition	Using all of your senses Suspending the cognitive mind
Curiosity	Flexible and open to change Receptive to environment Inquisitive and willing to not know it all

The first three elements relate to who we are and how our biology influences our response to the pressures of our lives. These include our instincts and strategies for survival. As we learn to identify our animal drives, conscious or unconscious, we develop the self-knowledge that we are our biology. As we become aware of how these drives influence the way we approach life and the decisions and judgments we make, the more choice we have in our lives. Learning about these three elements underlies the quest for self-responsibility in relation to the whole.

Like other social species, we have an innate desire to make a contribution to others. The touchstone for living a satisfying life centers on applying our natural gifts in the right place at the right time. It is invaluable to discover, reveal and nourish our truly unique aspects. As youngsters, many of our natural talents are invisible to us because they come so naturally that we take them for granted, not realizing that they are our gifts. Sometimes our educational system and families deny or discourage our gifts. It may take us many years to dust them off and finally own them.

Polishing our strengths and quirks (like polishing a gemstone) allows us to focus on what we are good at and feel a sense of accomplishment in our lives. Being able to contribute ourselves wholeheartedly to our tribe and community gives us an invaluable sense of satisfaction and provides a deep sense of meaning about our lives. As we learn to leverage our strengths and manage our weaknesses, we begin the path towards self-acceptance.

The latter six concepts comprise an integrated matrix of nonverbal communication. Being an animal, we sense others, we smell them, we feel their energy with these nonverbal communicators. Scientific research has shown that ninety-three percent of our communication is based on these body language cues (only seven percent of our communication is based on word content). These energetic cues provide the substrate through which we perceive others and, in turn, others perceive us.

Where one starts and the other ends remains a mystery. Perhaps there is no absolute distinction, one from another. Trust is built and maintained. It is broken and repaired. Authenticity is the barometer of emotion and is fundamental to finding peace and balance in life. Confidence comes and goes as mentioned in Sandy's story in the chapter *The Leader's Path*.

Confidence connects our intentions to what we care about as we ride the peaks and troughs of our lives. Intention is our life force, what we are passionate about. Intuition is ever present whether we listen to it or not. And curiosity is a mood that encourages our imagination and continues to reinforce our vitality: a joy in living.

A journalist once asked me if a leader could have some of these qualities and not all of them. Which one is more important than the others? Or which one comes before the others? Leadership excellence through varied terrain of our lives relies on each of these elements. A leader can be effective with some of these qualities and achieve success up to a point, but to excel to the next destination requires developing the other areas. Knowing when to express one quality more than another depends on the circumstances and our overriding goals. With these principles in mind, let's ask the question, "Are you leading your life or is it leading you?"

PART 2

ARE YOU LEADING YOUR LIFE

OR IS IT LEADING YOU?

LEADERSHIP AS FOLLOWERSHIP

The greatest danger is that we will wake up one day and
find we have not lived our own life, but someone else's.
—David Whyte

The small herd of horses moved gracefully around the arena. The lead mare was in front galloping effortlessly and with a beauty of movement that would inspire any living creature. The woman in the center of the arena directed the horses down one end of the arena, moved in front of the lead mare and asked the herd to change direction. They responded to what seemed like some invisible cue as they spontaneously slid to a stop and whirled in the other direction.

As the woman in the center became still, the lead mare responded by running towards her as if following her energy to a point in the sand. The woman stood her ground as the horse stopped just in front of her, presenting her face to accept her into the herd. The woman took a deep breath and stroked the mare. The mare exchanged a breath in return.

The woman followed the horse as she moved down the arena and just as simply the mare followed her. They were one, connected by an unspoken agreement that they were working together.

You could say that the woman was bringing the mare to life by inspiring her to be beautiful and powerful. And it would be equally true that the swift, concise movements of the mare inspired the woman to share her spirit and talents. Together they created a presence that caught the attention of others, horse and human, and began to bring *them* to life. How did the woman compel the horse to move? She hadn't spoken a word or cracked a whip.

The horse didn't know that the woman was a successful entrepreneur. The ease with which the horse accepted her influence didn't have anything to do with her title or high IQ. The horse simply found clarity in the woman's "presence"—she was *focused*, she was *confident*, and she was *willing to follow through*. Her leadership was not comprised of wishful thinking or hopefulness. Her extension of spirit and purpose created an energetic aliveness. Without needing words her presence said, "We *are* going this way, what we are doing *is* important, and at the end of the day we *will* be successful."

She was declaring the future by sharing her vision—her *for the sake of what* they needed to be a team—and she was embodying the confidence and commitment required to make it happen. She was not second-guessing herself or worried about how she was doing or what others would think of her. She was believed that what she saw possible could happen and she was going to follow through until it did.

The horse accepted her leadership via subtle energetic and nonverbal communicators. The horse listened to her intention, openness, directness, confidence, and commitment because it was present in the woman's body. Humans, like horses, are inspired by a person's *presence*, their way of being in the world. A person who has presence:

○ Is aligned mind/body/spirit
○ Is focused on what she cares about
○ Honors her own gifts and quirks
○ Is open to other perspectives
○ Has an open curious mind and playful spirit

Her inner sense of self-responsibility is reflected outwardly as *authenticity*, in which her inner and outer stories about herself are congruent with what she cares about. She chooses how she thinks, acts and relates to the collective herd that she has chosen to be part of. She follows her path without self-doubt, embraces appropriate social boundaries and integrates herself with the various personality styles of the group.

FOLLOWING HER HEART

The woodpeckers tapped at the old oak tree as a new group of women came to the barn to learn about themselves through the eyes of the horse. They were part of a nine-day women's leadership program. Each group consisted of eight women from various places across the country that had come to this particular program to develop their self-confidence and relationship skills. Some of the women were housewives, mothers, and students, while others were career women. During the program they practiced uncovering old stories that no longer served them and calling in new stories of possibility.

As the women settled into chairs placed on the periphery of the round pen, I brought our first horse teacher, Angel, into the pen. Angel's chestnut coat glistened in the sun. She drew a deep breath, as if preparing to open her heart and accept the human who was about to enter her space. Over time I had come to deeply respect Angel's generosity of spirit towards her human clients.

Angel and I had worked together before. She was the horse that I had chosen for the women to work with the first time I had come to work at this particular ranch. The work with the horses had proven so successful that it had become a key component of the program. And so, I returned spring, summer, fall and winter to work with each new group that came to the ranch.

As Angel dropped into the collective energy of the group, she began to awe the women with her keen ability to reflect each person's inner workings. She had left some of the women and meandered to the other side of the round pen when they were not speaking from their hearts. She would magically appear by their sides as they began to reveal their inner desires, the places where their commitments to the future had energy and life. The women observed Angel become a dramatically different horse with each woman and began to realize that her presence reflected each of them in a profoundly unique way.

It was Gloria's turn to come into the round pen and inspire Angel to be with her. Angel liked her right away and stayed close by Gloria's side. Gloria was a mother of three and a career mom. She was in her mid-fifties and had been offered an incredible new job in Seattle. As Gloria began to make a declaration that she was going to move away from her family in Hawaii to pursue a good job in Seattle, Angel shook her head urgently side to side as if to say, "No!" Gloria tried again to express her intention to take the new job. Angel shook her head, "No." The observers held their breath. (The unspoken comment in the air was, "O.K., the first time might have been a coincidence, but this is getting pretty surreal!")

Gloria looked at me, shocked and scared that maybe the horse saw too deep inside her. I said, "Perhaps Angel is saying that you don't really believe that you want to move to Seattle." Angel shook her head up and down, "Yes!" Gloria said to Angel in a question, "I do not want to move to Seattle?" Again Angel shook her head in a yes response. Gloria gasped, "I don't want to move to Seattle! I want to stay in Hawaii and be close to my family!" Angel really shook her head yes this time, big up and down yes's.

Gloria took a deep breath, looked at the ground for a moment, and then looked directly at her group. A few tears streaked her face as she confessed that her heart was really with her family, but that she thought it would be a good career move to take the job in Seattle. Her heart wasn't in it. Gloria was relieved that Angel had helped her gain clarity about her real intentions. Now she could go home and really know that she was doing the right thing for herself and her family.

Gloria represents the dilemma of many modern women. There is a practical logic in pursuing the next career move because in our culture we are rewarded for *what we do for a living* as opposed to *how we live*. It would certainly look good on paper if Gloria had accepted a promotion higher up the corporate ladder. But in her heart she knew the sacrifice of being away from her family was too great.

Gloria made a powerful leadership move in listening to and subsequently being responsible for what really mattered to her. She was relieved to discover that leadership is not about how many badges one has, but rather about being authentic and on-purpose with what matters to the heart. With Angel's assistance, Gloria gained confidence to follow her own lead, instead of succumbing to the cultural paradigm. Following Angel's reflection, she had taken a huge step in becoming responsible for herself.

FOLLOWING THE PATH TO FREEDOM

Freedom is having the *choice* to lead our lives with clarity and purpose. Leadership, or lack of it, arises from how we guide ourselves through the changing paths of our lives. Are we attending to our concerns and taking actions to make our life turn out as we desire, or are we letting life happen to us? Are we living in a static state of complacency, or are we directing ourselves into the future? What is at stake when we are only *reacting* to the pressures of the world instead of *creating* our world? Who is at stake when we don't believe in ourselves?

Animals who are emotionally, physically and spiritually free embody a sense of self-responsibility. They know they are an integral part of the whole. They are not afraid of their own power to influence. They do not live in a moral world nor rationalize whether their actions or those of others are right or wrong, good or bad. They do not shame themselves or other herd members for past mistakes or failures. They simply live in the present. Their power lies in their ability to choose and to act for the purpose of staying alive. Each day requires a different degree of focus, stamina, determination, and presence. Each challenge is regarded from a *feeling* stance (How do I feel about this?)—As opposed to a *knowing* stance (What competency and tool should I apply to this situation?).

Humans, on the other hand, perhaps because of our language, can ruminate endlessly about our psychological point of view, as if by thinking about it for an extra hour or another year, we might figure it out and in doing so, become magically cured of our neurosis. Horses find this a most irritating psychodrama that has little relevance to how to survive in the short term. Why? It doesn't *mean* anything. There is no *action*, no decision to make, no path to follow. As revealed in Gloria's story they don't listen to what we think we *should* do or even *why* we think we should do it. They listen to the energy and intention of our core longing—that which is most important to us.

FOLLOWING THE JUDGE

As a culture, we have unwittingly become soft and unfocused. In schools we are relentlessly desensitized and conditioned to do what we are told, to follow the rules. We are told by constant media interventions that we need a vast array of material possessions in order to be satisfied with our lives. We are supplied with so many choices that we become overwhelmed, which becomes a vague feeling of uncertainty. Products are no longer made to last and so when a part breaks on our fax machine; it is easier and cheaper to just buy a new one. We feel powerless to take a stand for quality and we become bystanders of disharmony. When we feel powerless, we see power as "bad." This allows us to justify that our internal disharmony of powerlessness is acceptable. We rationalize that it would be bad to be powerful.

In this state of mind, the term "leadership" becomes emotionally charged. Leadership begins to look like domination or command and control rather than *leadership as followership*. We become fascinated with concepts of alternative leadership as a way of avoiding our own power and self-responsibility. The passive leader is seen as a good role model and the assertive leader as a bad role model. What is often lost in our fear of power is that to lead simply means *to direct in thought and action*. It also means *to follow the course or path of.* We have forgotten that if we lead ourselves effectively, others follow naturally and without struggle.

Perhaps we inherited our view of leadership from our parents and communities. We may think we have a healthy view of leadership, but I have seen time and time again that people get stuck in their lives because they have a distorted perception of leadership that does not allow them to take responsibility for their lives. This short case study depicts a woman whose unexamined view of leadership inhibited her ability to extend powerfully into her life.

AN OLD STORY—LEADERSHIP IS A BAD THING

Leanne was one of twelve attendees in a Leadership & Horses™ clinic being held in Boston. She had come to the leadership seminar to focus on developing a business model for a retreat center where people could come to get rejuvenated and refreshed from their complex lives. As we discussed the principles of leadership, she kept responding with "yes, but…" as if defending against the notion that it was her responsibility to lead her vision.

Thinking that perhaps her view of leadership was interfering with her willingness to take responsibility, I asked, "What does leadership mean to you?" Sure enough, she confessed that when she thought of leadership she thought of leaders like Hitler. She thought that leaders were controlling and dangerous to others.

The group held their breath in disbelief. Leanne went on to confess that she was gripped in a story that leadership was domineering and controlling, hostile even. She knew she was stuck in this narrow, contracted view of leadership and was hoping to find a new interpretation that would allow her more control of her life and ambitions.

Leanne explained that she was a spiritual woman who could only rely on her intuition to guide her. The juxtaposition of her spirituality and her Hitler notion of leadership had become a personal prison. Her facial expression was desperate.

Leanne admitted that she knew what her problem was, but she didn't know how to change herself. She kept saying that she needed someone to help her, to tell her what to do. Without saying it, she wanted someone else to be responsible for her. She masked her unwillingness to be responsible for herself in her confession that she was stuck.

Knowing that talking with her would not shift her interpretation, I sent her into the ring to work with Pearl, a white Arabian mare. I asked Leanne to make a "declaration" of leadership—something she would be responsible for. She responded that she would like to work on her male side, which she felt was her negative, domineering side. I suggested a re-interpretation that it was not a gender issue, but rather her assessment of what leadership looked like to her. She insisted on staying with her interpretation because she felt it worked for her.

Interestingly enough, when she went to work with Pearl, a new persona, previously hidden, presented. Leanne turned into an overly aggressive contortion of energy. Her face was pinched and mean. Surely the way she had been treated as a child was reflected in every muscle and written on her face like a hieroglyph on a rock. It was as if she was Hitler herself. The horse became frightened and ran away from her in a dramatic flight response. It was painful to see Leanne embody her own dreaded interpretation of leadership and refuse to be responsible for it. The pain in the arena was so strong that the other participants fought back tears.

I gently asked her to relax her forehead, relax her face, use her peripheral vision, and focus on quieting herself. As she quieted herself, the horse quieted down. As Leanne returned to the group, tears streaming down her face, she apologized for herself.

We all witnessed the torture that lived in her body. She was still asking for help, saying that she had had enough of herself. Not only was she stuck in a negative view of leadership; she was struggling with a negative view of herself.

I asked her to tell us what she thought she did well with Pearl. It was very hard for her to come up with any positive

74

interpretation. She felt she had done poorly and was gripped in a self-deprecating story.

Leanne's notion that leadership meant that she had to be an overly dominating force through intimidation and anger lived in the physical memory of her body and so had to be addressed at both the intellectual and physical levels. Her story illustrates how our view of leadership can drive us into feeling victimized and powerless. Her view of leadership meant that one was either the dominatrix or the subordinate. In avoiding being a leader of her life she became a victim prone to feeling subordinate and inferior.

Leanne required several sessions to deconstruct her negative self-view before we could even enter into the conversation of how she was leading her life. We addressed the notion that power is the ability to *influence* rather than *force*. Being powerful is not a moral issue. It is neither right nor wrong to be powerful.

Power is having the choice to take a stand for meaningful issues and to act on that choice. Leanne had to learn how to identify the choices she was making in her life before she could be fully responsible for acting upon them.

When we confine ourselves to limited possibility, our intuitive side has no place to enter. It is as if our thinking mind, rationalizing its way with stories and agendas, clogs the vessels of our sensate longing. We move away from life's dilemmas out of fear of not having the right answer. We create mental stories to defend ourselves from the anxiety that comes with freedom.

THE LEADER'S PATH

If your actions inspire others to dream more, learn more, do
more and become more, you are a leader.
—John Quincy Adams

Humans did not invent leadership. It exists throughout the animal kingdom as a practical way for social animals to communicate, negotiate, and collectively contribute to the survival of the individual and the whole. As soon as two social beings, horse and human, begin to relate a powerful but subtle nonverbal negotiation begins. This need to know who is leading is instinctive for both humans and horses and also happens between humans but is less obvious. The nonverbal conversation goes something like this: *Who is leading? What are we doing together? What are we communicating? What needs to be negotiated? What is my role? What is your role?*

Working with horses and simultaneously practicing our leadership presence provides a rich opportunity to refine our natural talents and develop new skills needed to get us to our next destination. We deconstruct our limiting ideas of leadership and learn that everyone within any social context has leadership responsibilities. Returning our senses to our herd-like nature is not a sign of weakness, but a place to gain personal power through self-knowledge and acceptance. As we gain wisdom we increase our ability to contribute outwardly to the greater good.

The horse insists that we stay centered on what is important to us. Without clear leadership, the horse quickly becomes bored, frustrated and disinterested. A frustrated horse may begin to wiggle and toss its body around as if declaring a breakdown with its body language alone. A bored horse simply quits and becomes a thousand pounds of unmovable flesh, the epitome of a lackluster employee responding to a bossy leader who forces results.

The horse teaches the bossy leader to learn a new way to lead—with encouragement and inclusion. The cheerleading leader learns from horses to have constructive boundaries and set clear conditions of satisfaction for the team. The appeasing leader learns how to take a stand and direct her team with intention and assertiveness. The coach learns to guide clients, as opposed to following them around. The pull-along leader learns to delegate and -trust their team.

The leader's path begins with staying open and curious to the imagination, and having the confidence to walk into the unknown territory that is our choice to forge. Being connected to non-human members of the natural world reminds us that we do not have to be driven by our mental judgments or habitual thoughts. If we reinterpret what we are feeling as energetic information like horses do, we can detach from the story that this energy is negative in tone.

In this revised interpretation of our somatic experience, frustration is actually an increased sense of energy. How we interpret this energy and apply it in our lives is up to us. If we *choose* to see frustration as bad, then we may miss the opportunity to leverage its energy into a new and more positive direction. We collapse into a judgment that something is wrong with us or out of alignment. The energy of frustration merely signals us that some aspect of our somatic experience, mind/body/spirit, is not thriving. When we label an increase in energy streaming through our body as anxiety, we become fearful and try to push it away. Another option is to see the energy of anxiety as pure energy, fuel that can inform us and guides into new action.

The opportunity to choose how we respond to these energetic perturbations can only be accomplished by turning off the inner judge's chatter. Mary Oliver's poem, *Wild Geese*, exposes the judge and invites us to *feel* our way to our heart's longing.

"You do not have to be good.
You do not have to walk on your knees

For a hundred miles through the desert, repenting.
You only have to let the soft animal of your body
Love what it loves."

I have witnessed that the single most limiting factor to a person's feeling of success is our human habit of negative self-judgment. When our internal judge has its grip, we lose confidence in ourselves. It feels as though we are *walking through the desert for a hundred miles, repenting.* We forget what we are naturally good at and instead focus on what we are not good at.

Ninety-eight percent of the women I work with live in a story that they are *not good enough.* In this constricted state of mind, we become preoccupied with stories about the way things should be, distinct from the possibility that the soft animal of your body *already knows* what it loves.

How do we learn to let *the soft animal of our body love what it loves?*

Peter Kaustenbaum speaks eloquently about this part of the leader's path in the following interview in 2000 *Fast Company:*

"The problem is, when you are stuck, you're not likely to make progress by using competence as your tool. Instead, progress requires commitment to two things. First, you need to dedicate yourself to understanding yourself better—in the philosophical sense of understanding what it means to exist as a human being in the world. Second, you need to change your habits of thought: how you think, what you value, how you work, how you connect with people, how you learn, what you expect from life, and how you manage frustration.

Changing these habits means changing your way of being intelligent. It means moving from a non-leadership mind to a leadership mind. Authentic leaders have absorbed the fundamental fact of existence—that you cannot get around life's inherent contradictions."

He goes on to say:

"The leadership mind is spacious. It has ample room for ambiguities of the world, for conflicting feelings, and for contradictory ideas...leadership is the existential paradox of holding yourself one hundred percent responsible for the fate of your organization, on the one hand, and assuming absolutely no responsibility for the choices made by other people, on the other hand."

Peter's words sound simple, but what he offers is a lifelong journey towards wisdom and ultimately towards freedom. He invites us into the notion that leadership begins with unsentimentally examining and challenging our notions of the box we inherited, placed ourselves in, or simply fell into. He understands through his own experiences and educational knowledge that it is up to each of us to find our own path through a process of learning and becoming.

George Leonard, in his book *Mastery*, refers to this process of learning as the practice towards mastery, which he defines as *staying on the path*.

"How long will it take to master aikido?" A prospective student asks. "How long do you expect to live?" is the only respectable response. Ultimately, practice is the path to mastery. If you stay on it long enough, you'll find it is a vivid place, with its ups and downs, its challenges and comforts, its surprises, disappointments, and unconditional joys. You'll take your share of bumps and bruises while traveling—bruises of the ego as well as of the body, mind, and spirit—but it might well turn out to be the most reliable thing in your life."

George Leonard invites us into the notion that leadership is a practice that we *mature into* as we progress in life. What is important to us changes throughout our lifetime. Change is as constant as the sun rising and setting each day. Being aware of *how* we apply ourselves to our changing circumstances gives us choice and power.

In this process of *becoming*, it is natural for a leader to succeed to a point of limitation. We begin our leadership path with the natural talents and quirks we are born with. These virtues take us through various levels of success. When we contribute ourselves wholeheartedly we reach our goal only to find that we need to reinvent ourselves once again.

At this new crossroad we realize that leadership is not some end-game destination, but rather a path that we mature into as we grow and change. We can acknowledge our success and look at what new skills and competencies we would like to develop to get to the next place in our lives. We ask ourselves:

a) *What are my natural strengths that I am not leveraging effectively?*

b) *What are my current perceptions, thoughts, behaviors that may be holding me back from being authentic and making this transition?*

c) *What have I perceived as a limitation that may be a strength in disguise?*

d) *Based on where I say I want to go, what new perceptions, thoughts and behaviors do I need to develop?*

REINTERPRETING THE *I AM NOT GOOD ENOUGH* STORY

It was a beautiful spring day when Sandy stepped into the arena to work with Jet Star, a young mare in Lacey's herd. The breeze was soft as Jet Star stood listening to Sandy's leadership goals. Sandy had successfully founded a small, service-based corporation that recycled printer cartridges. Now, five years into the business, she was managing fifteen employees and could no longer manage all of the aspects of the business on her own.

Sandy knew she needed her managers to become fully responsible for their departments. She embodied a style of leadership in which she was performing alongside her managers. Sometimes this worked, but often she unintentionally took over her managers' projects, which left them feeling incompetent.

Sandy felt burned-out and increasingly unsuccessful as a leader of her team. She was losing confidence. She realized that she was no longer leveraging her unique talents of creativity and strategic thinking. Instead, she was caught in micro-managing the daily operation of her company. She knew she needed to cultivate her managers' abilities and willingness to maintain daily operations in order to free herself to focus on business development and strategy. She knew that working with horses would give her fresh, untainted insights into what skills she needed to build to be a highly effective leader of her people and company.

Sandy asked Jet Star to become part of her team and to perform a lunging circle (large circle) at the walk and then the trot. Jet Star easily moved forward for Sandy. Yet Sandy looked stern, as if things weren't working out so well. I was surprised by her lack of recognition of her effectiveness with Jet Star.

"Are you satisfied with Jet Star's performance?" I asked.

"Not really," she replied.

"What's missing?" I asked, baffled.

"I feel like I am still auditioning," she confessed. "I'm stuck in a story that I am not good enough."

Her team members, who were observing her leadership presence with the horse, were stunned. Sandy was making it look easy to move Jet Star around. Some of them had not been nearly as successful and they could not understand her lack of satisfaction of both her and the horse's success. Without Sandy's acknowledgement of what was working, Jet Star began to slow down and become less interested in pleasing Sandy. Jet Star was saying with her movements, "I'm not sure I am doing what Sandy wants, so why work so hard?"

During the debrief, her team expressed that they felt like Jet Star. They were not feeling successful because they weren't getting feedback from Sandy. They were doing what they thought they should be doing, but they were becoming slower and less effective.

Sandy began to realize that by not acknowledging her own success, she was letting her team members down. If she wasn't acknowledging herself as mirrored in the success of the company, then how could they feel success? Through her experience with Jet Star, Sandy committed to a regular practice of acknowledging her successes and the successes of her team.

Over time her staff began to thrive and, on their own initiative, take more responsibility for their work. Sandy also saw that by acknowledging what was working, she was able to let go of the urge to push her way through things and exhaust herself in the process. Her self-perception gradually shifted from focusing on her weakness to leveraging her strengths. In so doing, she began to feel a new sense of creativity and inspiration with her business. Her self-confidence rejuvenated and, in turn, inspired her staff.

FEAR AS A BIOLOGICAL DRIVE

Anxiety tips us off to the existence of our freedom:
It reminds us of our huge responsibility to
Choose who we are and to define our world.

— *Sören Kierkegaard*

A good friend and expert in the Enneagram who was trying to "type" me once asked me what I was afraid of. At first I nonchalantly responded that I was not afraid of anything, but as I reflected on the question, I was shocked to realize that I was afraid of *everything*. With new awareness of my multitude of fears, I wondered why I had given such a certain answer to my friend.

Upon further consideration, I realized that I incorporate my fears into a rich inner self-awareness. I have regular conversations with my fears, almost at a subconscious level. When I am fully aware of my mind/body/spirit and how I am responding to the environment, I choose how to respond to fear, instead of being driven by it.

There are times when I can feel the animal part of my body responding to a person or something in the environment with big internal sirens, saying "Danger! Danger!" By developing an awareness and emotional intelligence about my body's response, I have learned to take the time to think about how I am feeling and what my choices are distinct from rushing into a reaction.

Choice follows awareness. Choosing our response, rather than mindlessly responding to people and situations, increases our range of choices and thus increases our ability to move powerfully through our lives. The enemy to choice is fear.

Fear lies at the root of our insecurities and unless we face it head-on, we risk living a mundane life. Fear for our own survival is automatic and basic. Some fears are practical and realistic. But often, we are driven by sub-conscious, ungrounded fears that are old and inaccurate. Richard Leider and David Shapiro in their book *Repacking Your Bags* say:

> *"Nowadays, what most people feel when they don't feel anything in particular is fear. It's easy to see why. The world is a frightening place…Television, movies, and radio talk shows all remind us to be scared."*

One of the main fears, Leider and Shapiro explain, is the fear of having lived a meaningless life. What is a meaningless life? Perhaps it is a life not lived to its full potential, a life in which we didn't fully come forward with our passions, our talents—a life in which we did not recognize and honor our ambitions.

Peter Koestenbaum continued in the *Fast Company* article:

> *"One of the gravest problems in life is self-limitation: We create defense mechanisms to protect us from the anxiety that comes with freedom. We refuse to live our full potential…We limit how we live so that we can limit the amount of anxiety that we experience….*
>
> *No significant decision—personal or organizational— has ever been undertaken without being attended by an existential crisis, or without a commitment to wade through anxiety, uncertainty and guilt.*
>
> *That is what we mean by transformation. You can't just change how you think or the way that you act—you must change the way that you will. You must gain control over the patterns that govern your mind; your world view, your beliefs about what you deserve and about what is possible."*

Fear is a basic part of living, a biological necessity for survival. Where we humans fall short is in *not realizing* that we are afraid and subsequently not knowing *what* we are afraid of. This underlying animal fear for survival drives us unknowingly and, unless examined, becomes a contraction away from life. For those of us who habitually think *it's never enough*, the real question is *what are we really afraid of?*

Considering ourselves to be so highly evolved, we have developed extensive systems to pretend that we are somehow beyond this most primal fear. We like to insist that we are not driven by fear like wild animals are. Even for those of us who have distanced ourselves from discomfort, our primal fears persist underneath our veneer of ease.

If we look into the animal kingdom, we see fear is alive and well among the various species. A profound alertness for safety versus danger is any animal's greatest defense tactic for survival. Wild animals that are starving are dramatically more afraid than animals that have adequate sources of food and water. An undernourished animal becomes dangerous because it is in a heightened state of fear for its own survival.

Many people in third world countries don't have enough food to eat or water to drink. They are in daily fear for their survival. Most of us no longer remember how hard it was to actually grow or gather enough food for ourselves through an entire year.

We have so much readily available food to eat that we have forgotten how seasonal edible wild food actually is. We have also forgotten how many cans of food our grandmothers prepared to keep her family fed through the winter and, more importantly, how long it took her to put that food up. It takes me all day to can twenty-four pints of tomatoes. This does not include all the time it took me to grow and harvest the tomatoes. Twenty-four pints of tomatoes yields approximately twelve meals for my family of tomato sauce alone, to say nothing of the rest of the meal.

In *Into the Wild,* John Krakauer reveals the harsh reality of trying to live in the wild by telling a true story of how one young man ultimately starves to death because of his naïve and romantic notions of living off the land.

Surviving as hunters and gatherers like our ancestors was a full-time job. Imagine living in the forest with no running water, no house. Your entire day is occupied with gathering food, repairing your shelter, finding and storing water, making and repairing your clothing, protecting your resources from hungry marauders (including bears and other humans). Now imagine doing this alone. What if you broke your leg? Without the aid of another human being you would slowly starve to death.

Even though most of us have all of the modern conveniences of meals ready-to-eat, filtered water and the like, the ancient story of what it took to find food and water lives on in our genetic memory, unconsciously contributing to our basic fear for survival. Being a social animal, the fear of isolation equals the fear of not being able to provide for oneself physically or emotionally. The movie, *The Castaway*, is a disturbing look into the pure terror of being alone. In the movie, Tom Hanks deserted on an island with no animals, creates a social context in bonding with a soccer ball he calls Wilson whom he talks to in order to stay sane.

Another important aspect of our social nature is our deep fear of being ostracized or excommunicated from the group. This translates into our modern psychological terms of *fear of abandonment* or *fear of rejection*. As a social animal, we are fundamentally terrified of being truly alone. Horses, also an intensely social species, are terrified of being separated from other horses. On a deep level they remember how impossible it would be to survive alone.

Many modern equestrians wonder why their horses are anxious and flighty. Perhaps it is because they are isolated in a stall away from their herd, which confines the horse to a chronic state of fear.

Like the horse, we are innately terrified of being separated from the herd. This fear drives us subconsciously, and if left unrecognized, can trap us into a fear of taking risks, of *being all that we can be* for fear of standing out. In all my work with individuals, this basic fear of being alone translates into a fear of trying new things, taking risks, speaking one's truth, being honest about feelings, and even sharing natural gifts.

The fearful litany runs this way:

"I'm afraid to contribute my passions and ideas because: people won't like me; people will laugh at me; I won't be accepted by others, they will think I am stupid; I might be wrong and then people won't like me…" and so on, and so on, around and around, ad infinitum, freezing all potential for movement and growth.

This internal fear of separation from the group becomes our "inner judge" who turns up the volume of its recurring chatter in an effort to rationalize away our fear of taking a risk. Our "inner judge" creates internal rules and stories about what we should and should not do. Left unattended, this judge seizes more and more of our inner landscape until we believe that we are already being separated out. The following case study provides an illustration of this point.

WHAT WILL OTHER PEOPLE THINK?

In the spring of 1999 a beautiful young lady named Sarah participated in a leadership course at the ranch. Sarah was an accomplished professor of literature at a large university. She had watched half her group work with the horses and now it was her turn. She came into the center of the arena her head to the ground, as if already ashamed to be herself. Her body language reflected her inner judge's voice, "Don't mind me. I'm not worth your attention".

She appeared unsure and apologetic. She seemed obviously fearful of how the other people would interpret her performance. She began to cry and beg her group not to laugh at her. I looked at the group and no one was laughing. She was off-center and gripped in a habitual conversation about herself that made her afraid to take action, any action.

"Sarah, what is happening for you right now?" I asked.

"I am afraid that people will laugh at me," she replied.

I was miffed. How could she be afraid of what other people think, she is already so successful?

Stella, her horse partner, was disengaged and standing quietly for lack of direction. I tried to pull Sarah out by challenging her story, "Who cares if they're laughing? It's your life," I whispered.

I had caught her attention. I could see her thinking.

"I don't see anybody laughing at you." I said, followed by a question, "Do you?"

She looked at her group. As Sarah allowed her mind to disengage from its automatic fear, she saw that the observers were not laughing at her—on the contrary—they were engaged and supportive.

Stella's dull glance and lack of movement illustrated to Sarah that staying in her fear about how others perceived her was inhibiting her forward thrust into the world. Sarah could see that her fear of not being liked created a paralysis or inability to interact socially.

As she let herself breathe naturally, her fear dissipated as quickly as it had arrived. By becoming aware of her fear and the accompanying stories of her inner judge, Sarah was able to disconnect from her ungrounded fear. Her historic reaction had been to translate this sensation into a story that others were laughing at her, and that meant that she was outside the circle, lost and alone in some wilderness of her own making.

Now that her mind was no longer gripped in prejudgment about herself, we were able to focus on her commitment to write another book. Sarah allowed her body to *become* her ambition. She stood tall, her chest open, and moved from her focused presence to be a writer. She asked Stella to walk and trot as an expression of her commitment. Stella responded with simplicity and grace.

Once she was able to feel her ambition in spite of her fear, Sarah began to attract Stella's interest. She was able to feel the difference between being driven by her biology and choosing to engage positively in the world. When she allowed herself to share her ambition with others, and not be so concerned about what they thought of her, Sarah was able to transform Stella into a vibrant presence that inspired the others in her group.

Many cults feed off the fear of being excommunicated; if you do not conform to the cult's rules, you are not only a bad person but you will also be kicked out. Even many personal development organizations and horsemanship programs insinuate that if you do not accept and perform within their set of rules and ways of thinking, there is something wrong with you.

Participants in these settings (over the long term) lose their ability to think for themselves because they fear that the other participants and the instructors will reject them. They will stay in such unhealthy situations far too long because of their deep fear of being rejected or not included in the inner circle.

Many adolescents acquiesce to pressure from their peers in order to be liked or fit in. They often deny their own sense of right and wrong so that they will not be excluded. Youths that succumb to peer pressure often do not have a strong familial tribe (herd) to counter their need to be accepted by a bunch of other kids, or they reject the tribes they already belong to. They feel that their only choice is to acquiesce and betray themselves in order to be accepted.

UNIVERSAL CONCERNS FOR SURVIVAL
The ability of a species to survive is determined by the ability to reproduce and successfully raise offspring. A social animal's ability to reproduce is determined by how healthy each individual is and the group's ability to provide food, water and shelter to all of its members. Social animals depend on other members of the group to meet these basic concerns. The complexity of a species' social system is determined by how generously the habitat and its accompanying resources meet the group's requirements. Some social animals depend on specific territory to provide sustenance while other social animals are nomadic.

Fernando Flores, one of the major contributors to concepts of social interaction among humans developed the thirteen permanent domains of human concern. If we look at our instincts as a social animal, our universal concerns for survival are similar to other social animals such as horses, dogs, sheep, goats, etc.

Social systems throughout the animal kingdom organize around the need for the individual and the whole to take care of five basic concerns for survival:

UNIVERSAL CONCERNS OF ANIMALS
Food
Water
Shelter
Reproductive fitness
Care of young

At first glance, these requirements for living may look pretty distant to us, but they underlie the majority of our fears for the future.

A good friend of mine, a very successful businesswoman, has always owned a van. Her unexamined perception was that if the bottom fell out of her support system, she would still have shelter for herself and her daughter in the van. But as she became more successful, the van no longer reflected the successful woman she had become. She began to see that she was being driven by a historical fear of not having enough, a basic fear for survival. Upon evaluating her circumstances, she realized that she did, indeed, have enough, and did not need to live in her historic poverty mentality.

The majority of Americans live in a resource-rich economy. For many of us, we have an abundant supply of food, water and shelter. As our basic requirements for survival are taken care of, our biological drive to gather, hoard and store extends to excess material possessions, supplies and sundries.

We quickly forget that people in many places in the world spend every waking hour concerned about where their next meal will come from. Many people in Africa walk several hours each day just to gather water for their family. These people are not wondering who they are or what line of work they should be in. They are still taking care of the basics required to survive and raise a family.

An interesting commentary about the difference between the United States and many third world countries is that the United Nations Treaty stands for the issues of food, water and shelter for all, whereas the United States Treaty stands for independence and equality for all.

LIVING INTELLIGENTLY WITH OUR ANIMAL NATURE

When we observe fear as a natural process--a system of self-preservation arising from our animal nature--we can have a healthier dialogue regarding our instinctive fears. Rather than thinking that there is something wrong with who we are at our core or letting our judge create inaccurate interpretations of our pulsing aliveness, we can examine our fears and ultimately choose which fears are reasonable and which are over-estimated. By observing and respecting our animal nature as a product of our biology, we learn that our physical body responds before our mind even has a chance to reason or understand our situation. We learn that perhaps the increase in sensations streaming through our body is not fear of rejection, but rather fear of aliveness. Fear that we are the ones we've been waiting for, that we are ultimately the ones responsible for how our life is turning out.

Though it may seem that avoiding our true passion and

playing it safe is a practical solution, the risk is living a life designed by unrecognized fears about the *way we should be* distinct from living the life we are destined to manifest. The fear that we will be outcast if we think independently and follow our passion creates what many thought leaders call "The False Self." Mary-Elaine Jacobsen, in her book, *Liberating the Everyday Genius*, writes:

> *"A predictable life of few risks may be fine for many people. But it sounds like a death sentence to the Everyday Genius, who is designed for change. Nothing about taking risks is easy. Often we have to go it alone while others remain on the sidelines shaking their heads. So how do we get off the bench and into the game of risk? For starters, we must ask ourselves two pivotal questions: "What am I afraid of?"— Embarrassment, loss of love or respect, feeling like a loner, making a mistake, becoming powerless? — And "Can I ever hope to fulfill my dreams if I hang back and take no risks?"...The same risk that makes us tremble is also the inevitable traveling companion who accompanies us as we journey toward our hopes and dreams."*

Identifying our fears and subsequently challenging them allows us to create new stories of opportunities versus fearful outcomes of failure. For example, the fear of making a mistake is challenged by asking the question, "So, if I make a mistake, what is the worst that will happen?" Often the answer is, "Not much. I'm not going to die. I can recover from my mistake." The fear of social rejection is met with the challenging question, "Who will actually reject you and how much does it really matter?" Often, when we challenge our fears we see that they are largely ungrounded fantasies holding us back from living fully and unapologetically.

How do we get to know our fears? First, we learn to bring forward and challenge the mental chatter, the storyline that goes with the fear. We create alternative possibilities, encouraged by new stories of success and fulfillment. In addition, we notice how our animal body feels in relation to the fear. Sometimes in this particular practice, we realize we are not afraid at all, we are just experiencing an increase in energy that we mislabeled as anxiety.

We practice noticing our experience before we apply a story or interpretation. We identify our pattern of response to change in our environment. Over time, as we notice ourselves in an automatic response to change or conflict, we can detract the judge before it can take over. We notice our heart rate increasing, or our blood running and we say, "Wow, I am so alive. What are my choices in how I would like to respond?"

OUR ANIMAL RESPONSE TO CHANGE

Like the animals that are our totems of power, we display three predominant responses under pressure. In the natural world with her all-encompassing and unsentimental directness, change is inevitable. One moment the local environment is quiet and tranquil, the horses grazing peacefully. The next moment a change occurs in the environment. It could be other animals approaching, a change in the weather, a sudden noise. The horses and other local wildlife sense an energetic change, taking note of its tone and quality. The animals make immediate interpretations of safety versus danger and may even appear to freeze before responding.

The three automatic responses to energetic perturbations are to *take flight*, to *fight* or to *appease*. Different situations may require different responses. These responses may look like choices, but different animals/humans have different predispositions to one of the three responses as a general or unspecific response. If you put a horse in a round pen, most will run as if to flee, but if pushed to extreme fear will begin to fight or appease. If you put a coyote in a round pen and chased it around it would probably flee first and then try to fight.

We human animals have the same automatic responses to the varying pressures and energetic changes in our daily living that wild animals do. These responses are instantaneous and can also become conditioned over time to be our predominant way of approaching any and all change. Mother Nature does not want all the animals to respond the same way. She wants variance. For some humans the instinct to flee will be more predominant, while others of us will have an instinct to fight or appease.

AUTOMATIC RESPONSE	COMMON EXAMPLES
Flight	Avoids conflict Moves away from pressure Disappears emotionally Physically leaves
Fight	Defensive Moves into or against pressure Challenges other points of view Looks for the fight
Appease	Makes nice Overly friendly Moves towards pressure Smiles even when scared or sad Can only tolerate pleasant conversations

We come into the world hard-wired to respond to outside events automatically and without forethought. We are further conditioned by our familial and social experiences until we embody a habitual tendency towards a particular response. For example, siblings in an abusive family in which the father is physically abusive may have different responses to the situation. Under the pressure of fear for survival, the *appeasing* child will develop a habit of talking quietly and reassuringly, putting flowers on the table and trying to create a wonderful, nice environment so the father won't get angry.

This child may also develop a perpetual smile, often smiling when danger is present or in the heat of conflict. The second child develops a habit of *fighting* with the father. This child moves into adulthood with a tendency toward walking into challenging situations, looking for confrontation and getting easily defensive as if ready for a fight. The third child may develop a tendency to *fleeing* or moving away from conflict. This child disappears emotionally and develops strategies for disappearing into books, the Internet or other fantasy related endeavors. As an adult, this person literally fades into the background in conflict or increased stress.

We grow up conditioned to respond to others in the same way we interacted with our family members, peers and elders. We repeat responses that worked in the past until we become habitual.

The *flight* response can be as mild as avoiding conflicts or turning away from pressure, or as intense as all-out *run-for-your-life!* The person in flight literally disappears from view. In a meeting that becomes intense, this person energetically fades away. The other team members may not even notice that this person has virtually left the room. Their body may still be there, but they are gone.

The *fight* response ranges from being defensive, to walking into the challenge, to actually fighting. A person whose tendency is to fight is on the hunt for what is missing from the picture. They commonly say, "Yeah, but...." If someone says they can't do something, they become determined to prove them wrong. They hate stereotypes. When attacked or threatened, they fight back even if they know they are going to lose. They can't help it; they cannot walk away from conflict. Conflict consumes all of their attention.

The *appeasing* person is committed to everything being nice and friendly. They tend to be outwardly social, always asking questions of others to get them in conversation. They smile even when they are failing. Everything in the world is *good*, at least on the outside. They don't want to hear that there is a problem or that things aren't working out. Appeasers are great mood setters, cheerleading others constantly, but they have a hard time speaking up when they are not happy or things are not working out.

By learning how we respond as an animal first, we can learn to direct ourselves rather than being in reaction. When we are gripped in an automatic response, we are *thrown off-center* and lose sight of what we care about in the big picture, as well as what is in front of us at the moment. We are *driven* by our emotions and feel out of control. We have stepped out of our leadership shoes and into fear. We become vulnerable to others who, being animals too, know how to push us off our center by pushing our buttons.

The ability to counteract our automatic response under pressure increases our choices in new and complex situations such as a new situation at work, a new boss, a new team, or a new horse. If we are aware of our natural tendency to shy away, become argumentative or defensive, or make nice, we can intentionally choose whether this response is appropriate, based on what we are trying to accomplish. We may decide that it would be better to take a different approach and wear a different attitude. It's our choice.

Once we understand how we initially respond to change we can focus on the nonverbal communicators of leadership and learn how to not be easily pushed around and manipulated by circumstance and situation. Being able to sense how we feel as an animal at any moment empowers us to choose how to respond, to stand our ground, and to interact with others from a solid foundation of understanding and acceptance.

THE INSATIABLE APPETITE TO BELONG

Many people have the wrong idea of what constitutes
true happiness. It is not attained through self-
gratification but through fidelity to a worthy purpose.
— *Helen Keller*

Horses are born with an innate desire to be part of the herd. A lone horse does not last long on the prairie, becoming an easy target for predators. It needs the protection of the whole herd to increase its chances of survival. In turn, the herd depends on each individual horse to contribute to the survivability of the whole. It is imperative for each horse to find its place in the herd. This desire translates into an animal that wants to be of service, accounting for the ease in which horses have participated in our lives for thousands of years. It is only through confusion and abuse that a horse loses this natural desire to cooperate and serve.

Humans are also born with an innate desire to be part of the tribe (herd). To be part of the herd means that we are a valued member and the herd needs our unique contribution to increase its overall survivability. The sense of *being needed* encourages a healthy self-image and an increased desire to be of service. Every one of us privately longs to be valuable, to be of service and have an identity in our greater community. This makes sense, since the more social value we have, the more likely we will be helped by others in a time of crisis. The instinct to contribute is so deeply rooted that it is difficult to locate in our cognitive thought process, but if we listen deeply, we can feel this drive deep in our body and in our subconscious mind.

As social animals, we need to *fit in*. There is nothing more satisfying than contributing to others and feeling "needed". Just like the workhorse, we wonder, "Am *I doing a good job?*" When our leaders and elders tell us we are needed and what we have to offer is important and unique, we thrive. When we aren't getting feedback that we're doing good work, we lose confidence in ourselves. The resentful horse or resigned employee is the embodiment of an individual who has lost her sense of value. She is not sure she is needed any more. She does her work, but deep inside she doesn't feel like she is part of the herd.

I've been on both sides of this equation. Working at veterinary hospitals in my early career years I experienced a few bosses who were tyrannical in their communication practices. I deeply admired their heart and skill in veterinary medicine, but I did not like their lack of social skill with humans. Within a short time, while I loved working with the animals and the daily activities of my job, I lost a sense of satisfaction in my work because I didn't feel like my value was being recognized. I became resentful and blamed my bad attitude on my boss's behavior.

It took awhile, but I finally realized that I did not have to sit around passively feeling like a victim to my boss's inability to offer praise. I could ask for it. I began to let my bosses know about all of the little things I had accomplished to improve the conditions of the hospital or the care of the animals. I learned to ask if the work I had done had produced value for them. I asked if there was anything I could improve upon. By keeping track of my accomplishments and contributions directly, I was able to feel a sense of value even if my boss was unable to acknowledge it himself.

As a leader of one of my first companies I later experienced the same resentment. I knew I was one hundred percent responsible for the success of the company and for my employee's sense of satisfaction. I made sure that they had clear expectations and worked hard to find the right place for them to contribute to the mission of the company by putting them into responsibilities that coincided with their natural abilities. I practiced rewarding their accomplishments. Over time, I began to feel stressed and un-appreciated.

I remember coming into work one day and had the where-withal to notice that my shoulders caved in and I turned my head down as I entered the office. For the first time, I was actually cognizant that I was losing my self-confidence. I couldn't figure this out at first. The company was thriving. Why then was I feeling so burned out? After much contemplation I realized that know one was acknowledging my accomplishments. The feedback was one way, employer to employee. I wondered why I was working so hard if nobody seemed to appreciate it.

Fortunately, I was taking a management program to improve my managerial skills and I realized two important things. One was that as the company had grown, I had fallen into a day-to-day managerial role rather than a strategic, panoramic role. One day, I was teaching one of my favorite principles to a group of leaders about knowing your leadership style and I saw myself on my flip chart. I am a starter type. I like the energy of creating something out of nothing, the entrepreneurial endeavor of risk and reaching for the impossible. Because I was managing the staff on a constant daily basis, I no longer had time to think panoramically or nurture the creative energy of possibility. With this new realization, I developed a plan to remove myself from the daily operations and create time for myself to strategize and develop long-range goals.

The second thing I realized is that when we find our selves frustrated or not feeling like we are producing value it doesn't mean there is something wrong with us. Switching the coin, it simply means we are no longer doing what is right about us. And thus, the pain of resentment or frustration is our spirit's cue to go within and re-evaluate our gifts and talents and make sure our daily contributions are utilizing these assets.

Dr. Mel Levine, author of *The Mind Matters*, talks about the direct correlation between juvenile delinquents and their lack of feeling that they belong or have something to offer. They are told that they are no good at school, and what they *are* good at (often art or sports) is taken away from them as punishment for doing poorly in language and math. They feel like they are no good and so they *become no good.*

Since many of us have become isolated from our original tribes and communities, this lack of belonging becomes a distant, unacknowledged longing. We don't understand why we feel separate and alone. Or, as in the case of many dot.com millionaires, becoming financially successful just doesn't satisfy the soul. By becoming aware of our biological underpinnings, we can bring this drive into the foreground and find a way to nourish it once again.

Being of value is an important concept for a leader of a team, an equestrian, and a parent. Encouraging the other people in our lives to express their unique traits outwardly to the greater good is satisfying on many levels. Mature leaders understand the importance of their team members being *on-purpose.* In the business book *Good to Great* researchers discovered that one of the differentiating factors in a company's ability to excel was the leaders' ability to *place the right people in the right positions.*

These leaders focused on finding each individual's natural gifts and putting them in roles that came naturally to them so that they could thrive. Rather than trying to fit a square peg into a round hole, they placed each person into roles that suited them as opposed to placing them in the job that needs to get done. This strategy increased each individual's feelings of self-worth, which, in turn, increased their productivity and overall contribution to the company.

WHAT DO I CARE ABOUT?

George was a handsome man in his thirties and was living the American dream: a beautiful and successful wife, a Porsche, a big house in Silicon Valley, an elevated job title, a cellar full of fine wine.

As he came out to work with Stella on the long line, he made a declaration of how much money he wanted to make for the year. His plan was to inspire this pretty black and white mare into a walk by his embodied belief in his goal. But Stella would not move forward when he directed her to walk; she did not believe him. She stood facing him with an inquisitive look in her eye as if to say, "What do you *really* care about?"

George felt flustered as he tried to find a declaration that had meaning to him. He worried that he was shallow, since his only motivation seemed to be about money. He knew something was missing. There was a burning feeling in his heart every time he talked about the money. He confessed that this was the first time he could acknowledge that the money he made was not satisfying something in his heart. He still wondered who he really wanted to be. He was surprised that he was even willing to discuss this out loud. The horse's persistent silence as he struggled to find meaning in his life had already taken effect. He knew it was pointless to ask her to be part of his team (herd) if he didn't even know what that meant.

He had achieved the American Dream, but it wasn't enough. A deep longing to contribute wholeheartedly bubbled below the surface. He realized that he no longer knew what he cared about. How could he turn this breakdown into a positive direction, a path that had possibility?

He began to talk about his interest in environmental causes and permaculture. Permaculture was a far cry from the information technology world he had participated in for so many years. His internal judge immediately shut down this new idea.

"How can you make a living in Permaculture?" the judge said.

"How much money do I really need?" he countered.

"Yeah, but what will your friends think of you? And think about how dirty you'll be and you'll never have time to wear your nice clothes." The judge continued.

He became clear that his leadership challenge was to answer the most important questions of his life: Was he going to listen to his spiritual desire to contribute to something far larger than the technology stream or was he going to listen to his internal judge about who he should be and what he should do? To whom and to what was he going to wholeheartedly contribute? He was missing his core reason for leading, his *for the sake of what*. It was apparent that his social energy and enthusiasm would easily carry him to success once he answered these questions:

- *Who is your tribe or community?*
- *Who do you care about?*
- *What are your natural gifts or talents?*
- *What contribution do you want to make to the greater good?*

Six months later I got an email from George. He was pleased to report that he had had left his technology job and had taken up permaculture. He became a leader in his neighboring community creating inner city gardens for youth to learn how to grow their own food. He made less money, but he was happy and on-purpose. He finally felt successful in a way that his Porsche and fine wine had not provided.

Since the tragic events of 9/11, I find that over 80 percent of the people I work with are wallowing in an existential crisis of meaning (up from ten percent, in the mid-1990s). They feel like they live on an *isolated island* of their own making. These people no longer find integrity with the cultural package they were raised with: that more is better, that it is a sign of success to consume a lot, that it is an every-man-for-himself world. Some are brave enough to leave their high-paying jobs and career titles to do what they *really* want to do. They are willing to go into the unknown territory of making do with less money in order to do what they love and to contribute their heart to the greater whole. Others are still asking, "What am I going to do with my great love and short time?" We are in the midst of a grand cultural paradigm shift in what it means to be a powerful person in the world.

LISTENING FROM WITHIN

It was a warm fall afternoon when I first met Sheri. She had scheduled a riding lesson. The barn was full of distractions the day she arrived at the ranch. Stacy was grooming her bay mare near the tack room and Jane had just finished working her yearling filly. I busily readied Sadie with a saddle for Sheri to ride on. As Sheri began to speak about herself, I realized that perhaps she had not come to ride after all. I suggested we sit in the tack room and get acquainted. She told me about her and her horse, Sterling.

"What would you like to gain from our work together?" I asked.

"I don't know. I saw an article in the Chronicle about you and it just seemed right to schedule a session with you. I have a horse named Sterling. He is an incredible horse! He has become a wonderful jumper and currently competes in Eventing. I don't show him, but I have him with a trainer who works with him and shows him".

As she continued she revealed that she was confused about what to do with her horse at the current barn he was boarded at. She lived in Marin and drove the one-hour trip up to Sonoma two times a week to ride him. She began to get tears in her eyes as she confessed that she was afraid to ride him.

"I don't know why I am afraid. I have always been a good rider. I used to compete myself. He is such a wonderful horse, I don't know if I should ride him anymore. But it is important for me to ride". More tears welled up in her eyes. " I don't know why I am so emotional about this. I just want Sterling to be happy. He is such an amazing athlete he should be on the show circuit."

"Who said he should be showing?" I asked. It seemed that she had an unexamined notion that just because he was a great show horse he should be on the show circuit.

"Well, the trainer thinks it is important" she replied.

"What do you, Sheri, care about? What kind of relationship do you want to have with Sterling?" I asked.

"You know, I used to show a lot myself. Competing was such an important experience for me. It taught me about focus and being assertive. Usually I consider myself to be an assertive person. I don't understand why I am so confused now." She

105

sighed. A few more tears later she continued, "I don't feel that confidence I used to feel. But I love to watch him be shown by this young gal at the ranch. And I really want to support the sport that I love so much that has done so much for me throughout my life. I love giving this young woman a chance to ride a great horse, but I think I have forgotten about me".

By the end of our first session, we got clear that she needed to think about what kind of riding she wants to do now and if Sterling is the best horse for her. We also uncluttered the notion that just because Sterling was a great show horse, it didn't mean he had to be shown. This revealed her realization that she was still afraid of Sterling, that perhaps he was too much horse for her. We also discussed that Sterling was her horse and that it was her choice to decide whether to show him or not. Just because the trainer wanted to show the horse, Sheri needed to make sure that she was taking care of herself and her relationship with Sterling. She realized how powerless she felt in speaking her mind to her trainer.

During subsequent sessions, she was able to unravel old stories about power. Historically she had grained a sense of power and accomplishment in showing. She was very dedicated to the sport of eventing and perhaps it was time to create a new story of how she could contribute to the sport and engage in it without being the one showing. She was redefining what it meant to be powerful and influential in the equestrian world. She also practiced being a stand for what she cared about and being able to have conversations with the trainer about how she wanted her horse trained and shown as opposed to being submissive and feeling powerless.

This last notion was a significant issue. Riders like Sheri give trainers so much authority that over time they begin to feel that they don't have a voice anymore. There is an unspoken agreement at many training stables that you do things the way the trainer says to without question. Of course the show trainer wants the horse to be shown. It's how he makes his living. When she listened quietly to Sterling, she got the sense that he didn't care whether hew showed or not, he really enjoyed the relationship. She decided, rather than forcing herself and Sterling back into the show ring, she would put her passion for the showing into supporting younger riders and sponsoring local horse shows. She practiced with Sadie standing up to the trainer and telling him that she had decided not to pursue a showing career for her or Sterling. Once she felt confident, she took a stand and was at once relieved.

FINDING A NEW HERD

Carol had been a successful speech therapist for over twenty years. She had three children and had been married for twenty-two years. At 49, she hit a roadblock. She had grown up riding horses, but over the years she had let that fall to the wayside. She tried taking on various other hobbies to wake herself up. As her dissatisfaction with her life increased, she left her husband in hopes of *finding* herself.

She became increasingly depressed by the fast pace of life in California and her lack of self-meaning. When her father died, it seemed like the end of her life. At his funeral in Minnesota she met an old family friend and they fell in love. The romance continued long distance until they decided to get married. She moved to Minnesota to be with her new husband even though it was hard to leave her children who were grown up and beginning families of their own.

Little did she know that this move would change her life for the better. The small town she now lived in was quieter and the pace of life a much easier fit for Carol. She bought a horse and made new friends who rode their horses often together. She set up a therapy practice and quickly became an important member of the community. Her sense of purpose awakened her spirit and for the first time in years she felt needed. She had found a herd that appreciated her gifts.

Carol's story speaks volumes to the need each person has to feel a sense of belonging. No psychotherapist in the world could fix Carol's emotional angst, but reconnecting with horses and finding a place where she belonged gave her a new sense of well-being.

SANDY HEARS THE CALL

One could see that Sandy knew herself well. She had a calm, centered presence about her, and carried herself with ease and confidence. She exuded an air of self-reliance and at the same time, the other women in the group felt the care and support she proffered. Sandy had only recently been called to horses. She didn't own a horse or even ride. She wasn't sure why she had felt compelled to come to this equine-guided program on a warm fall weekend. Sandy had a feeling that the horses would help her learn something about herself. She couldn't explain it, yet she sat in the circle, like a chieftess ready to find the answers to an unknown something that was burning inside her.

Sandy introduced herself to the group as a minister of a nondenominational church in the city. She knew she was following her calling, but sensed that something had gotten lost. She no longer felt passionate at work. She felt burned out and unenthusiastic, but at the same time felt a tremendous sense of obligation to the church. As she negotiated the construction of a new facility she felt herself sundered by the internal dynamics of the church. Her traditional, workhorse mentality, to throw herself into her work; do what must be done—left her feeling isolated.

Her sense of responsibility to the staff and church members prevented her from telling anyone she was feeling dull and burned out. She didn't even tell this to the women gathered in a circle around her as, one by one, each shared her own story of self-discovery, unexpressed fears, and secret desires. It didn't occur to Sandy to mention it. Her job was to "hold things together." Or at least she thought it was. Sandy was stuck but didn't know it.

After hours of trying to explain why she was at this program, it was Sandy's turn to enter the round pen to share her story, goals, and desires with Lily. The six-year-old quarter-horse mare pricked her ears forward as Sandy walked through the gate into the round space. Sandy had seen how the mare engaged with the other women as each spoke from her heart about what she cared about, and what had meaning and life to her. As each woman walked toward the life of her choosing, Lily responded, sometimes walking next to the woman, sometimes walking behind.

Sandy sighed heavily as she began to speak. She told Lily about goals she *should* focus on, such as her commitment to create a new church that was bigger and brighter and could sustain the membership for a long time to come. Lily walked away. The women outside the round space didn't understand this. Sandy was a bright, engaged leader, why didn't the horse follow her? Clearly she was a seasoned leader and had made great things happen, but what was she hiding? What longed to come forth? Would she find the words to express something she didn't understand?

Sandy faced Lily and asked her to walk with her. Lily stood still, rooted to the earth. Her energetic extension into the ground was obvious. Sandy understood. "I'm stuck," she said to the group. "Lily is being me. I really don't want to be responsible for the construction of a new church."

An elder woman in the group asked her, "Forget about building a new church for a moment. What do you, Sandy, care about? What has life and meaning to you now?"

"I don't know," said Sandy. "It's the weirdest thing. I've never been here before." Sandy looked up at the sky as if looking for a clue. Perhaps deep inside she did know, but the truth that coursed through her body hadn't risen to consciousness. It still lived in the murky waters of an unknown landscape.

Just then, and nobody can explain why, all of the horses around the barn began to whinny: the new mare, Morgan, from her stall, Cowgirl in the south field, Billy from the west, and the nine horses in the field next to the round pen. They sang a crescendo of whinnies. At that moment, as the equine chorus resonated through the timbers of the barn and sent the pigeons flying, Sandy realized that the narrow categories of denomination, color, and creed present in the church had become far too limiting for her now. Something greater was calling her imagination. She just couldn't explain what it was.

All the women in the group sat in rapt attention. No one could deny this unique event. It wasn't feeding time—nothing around the barn had changed. Everyone had been introduced to the idea that horses listen to your inner longing, desires, and beliefs. They are a unique mirror of your inner voice, not who you think you are or who you think you should be. The horses reflect that inner calling that sends us forth into the world, sometimes on paths unbeknownst to us. Some of the women in the group that day thought that it was just a coincidence. Others had seen hundreds of different people interact with these intuitive equine guides. While it was impossible to explain what had just happened, they knew that it was a unique expression of Sandy.

The nine horses in the field approached the north end of the round pen and lined up facing Sandy, their ears pricked forward, heads raised. Superman stood in front, flanked by the others, their bodies touching looking directly at Sandy. All of the women gasped. Sandy turned to the horses, "What do you want from me?" she exhaled. She felt the afternoon breeze on her face and the soft sand under her feet and remained silent.

"Perhaps they are responding to something deep inside you, calling you forward," one woman said. Another added, " It doesn't look to me like they want something from you. It looks like they are acknowledging you in a very powerful way."

The first day ended in silent reflection. Sandy sat quietly at the south end of the barn. How was she going to give voice to what she felt inside? The soft animal of her body knew that she was done with her church. Somewhere hidden in her heart, she knew something larger was calling her, asking her to listen, asking her to believe.

Each time Sandy interacted with the horses over the next two days, a chorus rang loud and long through the barn, the arena and the round space. Morgan, Billy, Cowgirl, and the other nine horses called each other in an ancient voice, unified into one energetic field. Even the nonbelievers now believed that the horses were communicating something that the humans did not quite understand, at least not yet. And those who saw Sandy's effect on the horses couldn't deny they had witnessed something profound. Three different days, three different exercises and each time all of the horses within miles of here are calling to each other and gathering around her.

Sandy felt stunned and exposed. "I know that I'm being called by something, but I never imagined that horses could see inside me so profoundly. Now I know why I was called to come here, to this land, to these horses, at this time and place. I needed fresh ears and eyes to help me expand my spirituality. I'm tired of the nitpicking among different religious beliefs. I'm tired of the squabbles among the different denominations. I want to spend my time thinking beyond the past."

She hurried on as if making up for lost time, "So much of my work is about inspiring people to follow their hearts. Part of me as known all along that it is not the best use of me to stay at the church and build a new building." She took a breath. "So I guess its time for me to listen to my own words."

The elder woman of the group spoke," Can you share with us what your heart wants to follow now?"

"I want to open a new spiritual center. I don't know what it looks like, but I know if I take the first steps, it will become clear. I have that kind of faith." Superman whinnied, the women laughed, and Sandy felt a weight lift off her shoulders. Her body felt soft. A playful smile blossomed on her chiseled face. It was a good day to begin.

FINDING YOUR PLACE IN THE HERD

There is vitality, a life force, an energy, a quickening
that is translated through you into action. And because
there is only one of you this expression is unique. It is
not your business to determine how good it is, nor how
valuable, nor how it compares with other expressions. It
IS your business to keep it yours, clearly and directly, to
keep the channel open.

—*Martha Graham*

On a cold wintry morning I decided it was time to introduce
Cocoa to the herd. She had been living in a paddock next to the
big field where the herd of nine horses lived. She had seen,
smelled, and touched the other horses through the fence for several
weeks, as they did her.

Even with a fence separating them, a deep questing for her
place in the herd was already at work. All ten horses were trying to
sort out who was who in relation to each other. Even the herd
horses were back to the drawing board of how the hierarchy was
being re-established just by the simple addition of another horse.
They were each trying to figure out what this new horse meant to
the herd. *Where would she position herself? How would she relate?*

Being social animals, Cocoa and the other horses *needed* to
know how to relate to each other. Cocoa understood at birth the
importance of the hierarchal communication of the herd. Always
prepared for the impending predator, the herd needed to
coordinate instantly in relation to each other. In real time danger,
there would be no time to second-guess the decisions of the lead
mare. They simply would not have time to have a group
conversation in the heat of danger. They would not have time to

ask, "What do you think?"—"I'm not sure, what do you think?"

Cocoa knew that it was the lead mare's responsibility to determine how to respond and how fast to travel. The herd she was about to enter already had a clear system of communication in chaos. Lacey, the lead mare, had demonstrated many times that her aptitude for leading the herd was not granted by her size or heritage. She had proven consistently that she was more confident and persistent than the other members of the herd. She did not question herself or her ability to follow through once engaged in conflict. The other horses knew from experience that she did not acquiesce under pressure and her assertiveness was not a mask or false pretense.

As Cocoa entered the field the other horses rushed towards her. Lacey eventually approached with a challenging attitude; nostrils flared, ears pinned back. She wanted to know how Cocoa would respond to intense pressure. If she would move off when asked.

At first Cocoa backed away, showing that she was not interfering with the lead mare's space. A couple other mares came up to Cocoa and quickly turned their hind end in her face and kicked at her, again wanting to know how she would respond. She implied that she was willing to be influenced by the herd by backing away. As they persisted, she in turn kicked back at them and a fierce fight ensued. She finally felt a need to defend herself, showing them that she had her own dignity and was not going to be bullied. Over the next few days and many scrapes and bruises later, she found her place in the middle of the herd.

WHO HAS AUTHORITY FOR WHAT ROLES?

Each horse has its own personality, its own push into the world, just like people do. Some horses, like people, come into the world wanting to be in charge. They have a strong desire to be an influencer or director. Many more horses are satisfied with being part of the herd and influencing the whole from within. Still others aren't that interested in the hustle and bustle required to be one of the decision makers. They will wait at the outer edges for the heat of negotiation to settle down.

Observing herds of horses provides a visual playground for humans to learn the nuances of hierarchical coordination. At first glance the dominant mare and resident stallion seem to be the obvious leaders, each with their own set of responsibilities. The lead mare's obvious role includes choosing the best grazing land and productive watering holes, and maintaining acceptable social behavior among the herd. It is not her job to watch over every change in the local surroundings or fuss over minor matters. Instead she reserves her awareness to the big picture, conserving her stamina for the intensity of change.

At closer examination, it becomes clear that the lead mare's most important and primary role is that of *direction setter*. In danger or stress, the lead mare quickly responds with a decision about *what to do, where to go* and *how quickly to move*. The entire herd follows her without question. In danger there is no time for consensus or democratic thinking. She moves with determination and intensity and the herd follows with equal energy in the direction she sets. Perhaps this singular need for one director confuses the human into thinking that there is only one leader.

What gets missed in this interpretation is that there are several senior mares who are integral to the success of the lead mare and the herd as a whole. Often it's one of the other mares who senses danger first. These 2nd and 3rd mares communicate a sense of urgency to the lead mare through their heightened awareness as if to say, "what should we do about this sudden change in our environment?" The lead mare senses their concern and responds with a clear decision about how to respond.

The lead mare and stallion have different roles and responsibilities in caring for the herd. One does not lead *over* the other. They coordinate together inside of their different roles. The stallion's main role is to protect the herd from danger. When chaos arises, even the stallion refers to the lead mare for the direction of travel. The lead mare directs the path of travel while the stallion pushes the entire herd into a huddle of swiftly moving horseflesh. (Horses tend to pack into dense clumps as opposed to deer. Deer tend to scatter in flight.) The stallion keeps the younger horses in check and trains the future stallions in the physical prowess they will need to defend their own herds.

This hierarchical strategy is very important to the well-being of each individual in the herd and is commonly seen in other social animals. If a horse is too individualistic and does not coordinate with the herd, it becomes an easy target for the fast approaching predator.

What is often missed in observing herds is the important roles the other mares play in increasing the survivability of the whole. The lead mare needs feedback from the other mares about the ever-changing environment. The other members of the herd assist her from their vantage point and send cues to her about what to pay attention to. The senior mares often attend to the daily herd dynamics in more detail than the lead mare. Some pay special attention to raising the younger horses and teaching acceptable social behavior. These mares basically mentor the younger horses. Their care and nurture is how the nuances of coordination and communication are passed down to the next generation.

Some of the mares prefer to stay on the peripheries, alert for predators. They often get mislabeled as outcast or they just don't fit in. but actually, these mares are the barometers or sentinels of the herd. They are the first to see change on the periphery. In a sense they are the intermediaries and hold a vital role in the survivability of the whole herd. The herd would not thrive without each member of the herd applying their unique personalities and physical abilities. This basic realization that hierarchy is not the *one man on top* theory blows up our inherited view of leadership.

In the horse herd, the authority of the lead mare or stallion is never a given. It is not a static state of responsibility, achieved once and always held. Other herd members reassess the lead mare and stallion's status regularly. The next generation of assertive mares and stallions press upon them, asking, *"Are you sure you're the leader?"*

This turns out to be very important to the survival of the whole herd. The better the lead mare and stallion's leadership, the more likely their herd and all its members will flourish. If they did not have the other horses' feedback, they would not be forced to think ahead. They might think they are doing a good job, but their instincts would grow rusty. If they were to become complacent or lazy they would miss significant cues informing them of the changing habitat or resource availability. In doing so, the entire herd is at risk.

Hierarchy in its simplest form is a system of agreements made about who will do what. Each individual of the whole has a specific role to play in the survivability of the whole. In nature it is not intended to create a command and control system. What we often experience in human systems that create a bad taste in our mouth around the topic of hierarchy is actually an individual or system of individuals who are abusing their position of power. In a horse herd, the bully would not be followed.

Hierarchical strategies, like leadership strategies, are malleable and shifting. The need to communicate via a chain of command is neither good nor bad, right nor wrong. It exists regardless of what we think about it. Hierarchies exist throughout the animal kingdom in order to support survivability of the species as a whole. It is a basic requirement for effective coordination in social animals.

Social animals under high stress or danger do not have time to discuss who has more authority over whom. Or who gets to make the final decision. It's fascinating to watch even human groups of people silently making agreements about who is leading who.

When we look at our human familial and communal habits, we see an order of hierarchy in relation to age, social strata, degree of competency, etc. The questing for position in society is similar to the questing in horses for herd position. Many of us do not like to think of ourselves as hierarchical. Many more of us have automatic assessments that "hierarchy" is bad because we assume it means

117

that only one person has power. Perhaps the historic abuse of individualistic megalomaniacs in offices of power has distorted the concept that hierarchy is natural and pre-existing. To deny that hierarchy exists is shortsighted and unrealistic.

In Joseph Jaworski's book *Synchronicity*, Peter Senge discusses Robert K. Greenleaf's philosophy on hierarchy:

> *"Only when the choice to serve undergirds the moral formation of leaders does the hierarchical power that separates the leader and those led not corrupt. Hierarchies are not inherently bad, despite the bad press they receive today. The potential of hierarchy to corrupt would be dissolved if leaders chose to 'serve' those they led—if they saw their job, their fundamental reason for being, as true service."*

Horses and humans have a similar sense of hierarchy living in the sinews of their bodies. We can engage with horses because of this similar biological pattern. Sometimes we get in our own way, when we negate this aspect of ourselves. But if we can think of hierarchy as a conversation about finding our place in the herd; the tribe; the community; our natural desire *to be of service* (to the larger whole) can be fulfilled.

Further insights are possible if we think of a team of people like a herd of horses, a whole new playing field becomes visible. When a person is added to the team, there is a subtle posturing and challenging of this new person as the rest of the herd tries to figure out how this individual will fit in and what their personal boundaries are. Can they take direction well? Are they self-generating and self-motivated? Or do they need constant management? Will they think like a herd member or think only of themselves?

Research in human science has shown that a manager can only manage up to eight people. A band of horses, we commonly refer to as a herd, is made up of seven to eight individuals. A herd of wild horses is made up of several bands, much like our corporate hierarchy.

THE RIGHT PEOPLE IN THE RIGHT POSITIONS

Karen was the CEO and founder of a successful software company. She had attended a private Leadership & Horses™ program with a group of other senior level executives and had learned through her first experience that she was a self-starter, very generative and full of creative ideas. She decided to bring her team out to learn from the horses because she hoped to gain insights on the unique qualities of her team members. With this information she hoped to assure herself that each individual held a role within the company that leveraged their natural strengths.

Jet Star, a bay filly with a diamond-shaped marking on her forehead, was only three years old, but was already a "leader in training" within her own herd. Every time I would go out into the pasture to get one of the more senior horses she would be the first to approach. She would look at me inquisitively and follow me around. So, one day it just seemed like the right time to see if she was ready to work with people.

She greeted Karen with natural curiosity. It seemed as though she wondered if Karen might become a new member of her herd. Her biological need to understand her place next to Karen kicked in. As Karen asked her to move in a circle on a long line, Jet Star looked at her inquisitively as if to say, "Are you leading, or am I?" "Are you sure about yourself?" "Do you know more than I do about how to respond to the environment?"

Karen answered the question by clearly extending her energy and commitment to take care of Jet Star. Her enthusiasm for leading was contagious and the horse moved easily and with fluid movement. During the debrief her team members confirmed Jet Star's clarity of her leadership. They trusted her ability to lead the company and were fully committed to the direction she was leading them in. They were engaged with her goals to grow the company and were happy to be on her team.

Karen's worried that her staff wanted to be like her, but she knew that their ability to succeed was in each team member being at home in their particular role. She felt like they thought that they had to be quick thinking and strategic like she was. She already had a sense that their power was in other roles such as fulfillment and managing their own departments. As they took turns exercising Jet Star on the lunge line, it became clear that each member of the team had different strengths and limits. The office manager had a hard time getting Jet Star started. Jet Star stayed put in the center of the circle looking at him as if to say, "What do you want to do?"

The manager finally got Jet Star moving at a trot. And boy, was that trot beautiful. Jet Star traveled ground steadily and consistently. But each transition—from a walk to a trot, a trot to a walk—was awkward and disconnected. Jet Star had revealed through her way of moving that the manager was good at maintaining his presence once things were in full swing, but getting things started was difficult. He admitted that it was hard for him to take initiative on projects, but once he was given the parameters he was very successful at following through to completion.

Next the sales manager practiced leading Jet Star on the long line. Again, Jet Star hesitated in the center of the arena; happy to conserve energy until the young leader decided it was time to move. She was waiting for clear direction. Jet Star stood there looking him square in the eye, open and curious, as if to say, "What are we going to do today?"

Being an animal that conserves energy, she would stand in the center of the arena all day waiting for the new leader to provide her with a job: a purpose to perform. She patiently waited for him to give her a job to do. In order for her to accept his leadership he had to prove that he was confident and sure about himself. He needed to confirm that he could protect her from uncertainty by providing her with direction, the way a lead mare does for her herd.

Through trial and error, he finally embodied a sense of purpose. He stopped trying to think his way into leadership. He let the energy of his intention come to life and extended a sense of purpose toward Jet Star. The bay mare perked her ears forward and began to move around the circle. Her pace was slow, then fast, then slow again. With her body language she was asking him to get out of his head and stay with her.

By slowing down and speeding up she was reflecting his energy: present one moment, in his head the next. As he started to think about how he was doing she would slow down again. In essence, she was asking him if his senses were wide open: if he could feel the shift in her energy, if he was paying attention to his own.

Jet Star, like most horses, will offer 150 percent of herself, but she insists that we give her the same 150 percent of ourselves. As we ask horses to stretch into new levels of performance they ask us to stretch just as much. At the end of the day the team was able to reinterpret their own notions of hierarchy and were excited about reorganizing themselves in relation to what they were good at rather than what job needed to get done.

Karen realized that her executive secretary's pushiness was actually a good thing. She kept her on her feet thinking two steps ahead. She decided to give her more responsibility, which thrilled her employee.

During the debrief the team reinforced that the office manager was great with seeing projects through, but that he was not the person to put on the beginning of a project that needed jump-starting. He was relieved to know that he did not have to start new initiatives; his job was to focus on project completion and other operational details. His role as fulfiller and completer was essential to the success of the whole. His steady mood and consistent energetic focus (as reflected by Jet Star's smooth gait) was vital to balancing the other energies of the group.

If Karen stayed in her role as strategist (paying attention to the big picture), the other members could settle into their own responsibilities. At the end of the program, they felt like a herd of horses, settled in their places and knowing that they each needed the other's unique way of being to succeed as a team.

The team learned (through the visual example of their energetic rhythms as reflected by Jet Star) that they each had different strengths and that Karen had intuitively placed many of the members in the right positions where their natural strengths could flourish. They realized that it wouldn't be effective for the company goals to have five Karen's running around with a whirling energy of direction-setting.

FINDING HIS PLACE

The rain pelted the roof of the barn the day that Chip arrived at the barn. The humans were bundled in their down jackets, hats and mittens. The white trailer squeaked and churned as Chip riggled around trying to view his new surroundings. Nancy, Chip's woman, daintily stepped out of the truck and immediately went to the trailer window to reassure Chip with soft words.

I took off my mittens and extended her hand to Nancy in the familiar human greeting. "It's nice to meet you," she said.

"Yes, its nice to meet you too. I have heard so many wonderful things about your place; I am so happy that Chip can come here and be a horse again. He's a rescue. He's a bit thin and I have not been riding him since I got him. His mind was fried by his last owner who put too much pressure on him as a jumping horse. My hope is that he will regain his confidence, settle down and not be so high strung." Nancy replied.

As Chip backed out of the trailer, he took on a regal stance as if he was stepping towards his next winning race. He was well traveled. He had been a race horse as a colt, never won much, but had tasted the roar of hoof beats, the flared nostrils, the stretch of will. He smelled the other horses and let out a shrill whinny, which was met by a cacophony of calls as if all of the horses felt a sudden need to locate each other.

As Nancy led him up to the stable, Chip pranced and bounced, snorted and bayed. Once in his new home, Nancy fussed over him as long as she could and as the day became dusk, she got in her truck and headed home. Chip's entry into the herd was a study for anyone who noticed only the subtlest of details. I could spend a lifetime in curious fascination watching herd dynamics, knowing deep inside that there was always something new to learn about the complexity and importance of this social instinct.

Lacey, the lead mare, ran him down the field teeth bared, followed by Superman who ran faster and bit his rump. Chip bucked, took the bite, but was not afraid. He kept coming back to the herd as if to say *I want to be part of you.* After a few minutes, the herd decided that Chip wasn't a threat to their established order, and he could hang out near them, not with them mind you, just near them. Chip was happy enough to graze on the outskirts.

Over the next two months, Chip continued to hang out at the edge of the herd. The other horses still didn't see him as one of them. Even though he was not part of the herd, Chip had become very aggressive at feeding time. He would chase the Lacey and Superman off the hay. I was curious about this because no other horse had been able to do this before. As I watched one morning I noticed that while he could move the other horses off of the food, when it came time to go out into the field no one followed him or even included him. He would stay at the barn while the rest of the herd followed the narrow cut trail over the gully, down into the ravine and up the steep hill to a sweet plateau of grass overlooking the barn.

Most people would assume that Chip had become the lead gelding of the herd since he could push the other horses off the feed. Lacey's place as the direction setter was still intact. Superman's position as the lead gelding was unaffected by Chip's presence. Indeed, the herd seemed to dismiss Chip once their bellies were full. Sure he was a bully on the surface, but the other horses didn't respect him. They easily left him behind each day.

Chip's aggressive and bullying style worked during feeding time, but the herd did not respect him as a leader. They didn't even care if he was part of the herd. He reminded me of a bullying leader who uses an aggressive demeanor to get people to perform. His staff would go through the motions, but as soon as they had other options they were not remotely interested in following.

Over the next few weeks Chip began to follow them, but as he reached the gully, he would pause. I could see that he wanted to go to the lush field with the others, but something bothered him about the gully. I didn't think much of it until Nancy came to visit Chip.

"I'm worried that he doesn't go over the gully. Doesn't he want to be with the others?" She asked.

"He does seem lonely once they've left. But something really has him bugged about the gully. Someday he will figure it out, when the time is right for him." I commented as I left the barn. I wasn't feeling well so I headed up to the house to rest. I sat quietly looking out the window as Nancy haltered Chip and set out toward the gully encouraging the gelding to follow. She patiently walked over the cut in the path where the seasonal creek trickled downward on its determined path to the estero. The gully wasn't that deep, nor was it that wide. A small hop would suffice. But time after time, Chip would walk up to it, stop abruptly, back away, and turn around. Finally after two hours, Nancy walked up the hill to the house, knocked on the door and asked if I would help her get him over the gully.

I reluctantly accepted, put on the wrong shoes and walked down to the field. I tried several obvious methods of enticing him over the gully. After another half an hour, I stopped, paused, looked at Chip and realized that if I really wanted to make him go over the gully I could. But I simply didn't need to prove my ability to force the horse into something that I didn't have a big enough story about. I really didn't care if he went over the gully.

For perhaps one of the first times in my life as a horse trainer, she told the truth, "Nancy, you know, I could make him go over this gully. It won't be pretty. But I am lacking a really good reason to put him through a fight. There is something else going on here besides egos."

This was so un-trainer like. I wasn't quite sure whether it was because I didn't feel well or if my psyche was re-negotiating the traditional horsemanship model that 'you must make the horse do what you want, when you want it'. It just didn't feel right to make him get over his demon. At least not today and not in half an hour.

What did the gully remind Chip of? I wondered. *What memory did it spark?*

"Can you put his hay on the other side of the gully so that when he gets hungry enough he might go over?" Nancy asked.

I looked at his slim frame and despite my resistance I said, "sure."

But that evening I didn't have the heart to starve the horse beyond his demon. I called Nancy the next day and explained that she I decided not to taunt him the way she had proposed. He really needed to gain weight and that seemed more important than Nancy's desire to make Chip do something he clearly had some reason for avoiding. Life seemed to go back to normal around the barn. Each day the herd left Chip at the gully as they headed for greener pastures. And each day Chip would stop at the cut in the path and wait for their return.

I grew increasingly curious about Chip's battle with the gully. I thought of the numerous women who had attended my self-development programs and how they each had some mysterious *gully* they were afraid to cross. The gully being symbolic of some deeper fear; a reminder of one's vulnerability. The tender reward of lush greens lying just beyond the small leap of faith. Oh but the *leap*, how grand it seemed. The gap between here and there, the old self standing still, stuck in place, while the imagination grew rye and oat just out of reach.

What would it take for the fear to lose its hold: the fear of failing, of falling into the bottomless pit where the fabled monsters dwelled? What act of courage would it take to step beyond the known terrain? To allow the body to follow its own imagination?

A few weeks later Nancy had the vet out to examine Chip. She quietly held him in the breezeway as the vet ran his hands down the horse's back. As he reached the place on the spine where the hipbones begin their articulation, his hands paused.

"You see this area here, how the left and right side of his rump are not balanced. The right side is higher than the left. He has an old injury that prevents him from having normal flexibility. I see this often in jumping horses. You see what happens is the horse is heading over a jump and as he gets to the other side his front legs slip out from under him and he basically does the splits, tearing ligaments and tendons as he falls."

We finally knew why Chip wouldn't cross the gully. To get over the gully, Chip would have to re-enact the motion that caused his injury. The thought of jumping over the gully brought back the memory of the pain and humiliation of his past failure. Finally I could explain why it hadn't felt right to make him conquer his demon. He indeed had known better than we did how he needed to protect himself. I had faith that Chip would overcome his fear when his body was ready. Or when his desire to be with the others, to taste the sweet rye, outweighed his fear of falling. Either option was available to Chip. Perhaps if Nancy stopped trying so hard to push him, to require he get *confident*, his imagination could flourish and overcome the demon of doubt.

"Light riding will be ok for this gent, but no jumping Nancy," the seasoned healer commanded. And off he went to the next horse/human dilemma down the road.

A week later, I was finishing a ride and noticed the field horses heading for the upper pasture. For some unknown reason, I stopped what I was doing and watched as Sadie, one of the elder mares hopped over the gully followed by her son, Superman, and his son, Sunny. But what struck me on this warm morning was that Sadie turned around and looked back at Chip. The horses had not expressed care for Chip before. It seemed like she was saying, "Come on, you can do it."

Chip looked at her longingly. His desire to follow her was palpable. To my surprise Sadie went back up to the gully, hopped over it, nuzzled Chip, turned and hopped back, "C'mon", she whispered. She repeated this three times. Several other horses came back to chip's side, paused and then went over as if showing him that the gully was not so bad. He did not have to leap over it like a jump; he could step over it one foot at a time. Superman even stopped and stood right in the gully as if to imply that it wasn't really a gully after all.

Sadie tried one last time, looked up the field and began to leave. As she walked away from Chip the light breeze brought the sweet smell of the fields and before he could think, Chip lowered his head, sniffed the gully and walked over it daintily, his hooves grounding him to the earth. The gully held his weight and as he reached the other side he let out a gleeful buck. The herd, all of them now, cheerfully set their tails to the wind and galloped up the hill.

PART 3

THE NONVERBAL LANGUAGE OF
ANIMALS AND HUMANS

TRUST

*We may lie with our lips but we tell the truth
with the face we make when we lie.*
—*Friedrich Nietzsche*

The red-tailed hawk watched me closely as I stepped into his pen. He was recovering from a bullet wound to his right wing and it was my job to exercise him daily to encourage his healing. First I would massage his damaged wing, followed by a series of exercises that would stimulate his reflexive muscles. Then I would attach him to a fishing line and exercise him in flight. The goal was to rebuild his strength so that he could be released back into the wild.

But first, I had to catch him. The task of actually catching him was of paramount importance. If I did not catch him on first try, he might jump around his pen and damage a flight feather. It only took one damaged flight feather to push his release back another six months.

The longer a bird of prey is confined and caged the less likely he will remain releasable. So the stakes were high. If I was unsure of my ability to catch the bird, or if I was not completely focused on the bigger picture, I might actually be putting the bird in more danger than if I did nothing at all. On the other hand, if I did not attempt to catch him for fear of causing him harm, he certainly would never be released because his muscles had already atrophied in captivity, a condition that can happen within a three-week period and without exercise he would never regain his strength to fly free once again.

If I thought about catching him, he was gone. It was as if he actually thought faster than I did. If I thought to myself, *O.K., I am going to reach out and catch the bird now;* the hawk would fly away before my mind could think the 'O.K.' part. Shaman knew my plans before I had actually thought them through. I knew that if I was uncertain, he would become afraid and fly into the walls. If I did not trust the bird to take care of me, he would not trust me to take care of him. To catch Shaman I had to act without mentally preparing myself. I had to just *be* the hand reaching to connect, rather than *the mind thinking* that I was going to extend my hand and clasp his legs.

Many birds before Shaman had taught me how to be confident in my body, not to doubt or fear these majestic birds. I had to trust him in order to ask for his trust. Really *trust*, not think about being trusting. To embody this trust meant having a deep faith that he would understand my good intentions. A *faith* that he would hear my belief in his potential freedom. If I could hold this bigger vision of why he needed to trust me, perhaps we could forge a mutual path of reciprocity. To translate this faith on a nonverbal level required not thinking, not having an agenda, not applying my intellect. It required opening my heart and believing that we could communicate without words.

With eagles, physically stronger than I, the willingness to trust the unseen energies of communication became even more imperative. When I looked deep into their eyes, I would forget about their talons and beak so perfectly designed to tear flesh from bone. I would find the bridge of trust that I needed to forge. When I held images in my mind of them flying free over the fields, it seemed like they would soften and relax as if they could see my images too.

Many a bird came and went close to my chest, our eyes each looking into the life-force of the other, and it never ceased to amaze me how they seemed to know that I was trying to help them survive. How easy it was for them to trust me with their life. I always wondered why they didn't just go ballistic and try to flee or fight their way through such a foreign experience. It is a feeling one cannot quantify in any scientific metric.

They would relax into the healing process. They let me fuss

with their wings and calmly wait for me to put the flying gear onto their bodies. As I handled them, they would look deep into my eyes in such a way that I felt totally exposed as if they knew more about me than I did about myself. Their deep faith became an inspiration to me. If I could become like them, I would be all right in this world. I could trust that the answers were available in my own animal knowledge. I could trust my body to tell me who was safe and who was not.

I remember countless other times when working with coyotes, bobcats, and mountain lions, that they were so deeply in tune to my inner thoughts that I had no choice but to become aware of them myself. If I was not aware of my inner feelings, I was actually in danger. I not only had to read if the animal was safe, but if I was safe to the animal. If I was afraid, I was not trustworthy to the wild animal. Equally so, if they were afraid they were not entirely trustworthy either.

One crisp foggy morning as I walked the fields I came upon a coyote stuck in the fence. He wasn't just stuck; he was strung out like a bed sheet on a clothesline. Spread out and woven into the top wire of hog fence that separated my land from my neighbors. He had gotten his rear leg stuck in a trap designed to strangle him. As he had tried to jump away and get free he had somehow managed to tangle himself in the six by six inch squares of metal fencing.

I quickly went to my tool shed, got some wire cutters and a pair of gloves and headed back to the coyote. As I approached him I spoke in silence, "I am coming to set you free, to cut you out of the fence. But I need your cooperation. Will you allow me to come close to you?" as I got even closer and saw what a mess he was in, I realized this would not be a simple process. So I explained to him, "This will take some time and you need to trust me that I am here to help you and I need you to stay perfectly still." He responded with quiet recognition in his eye and I could imagine a sense of relief too. As I cut first the wires around his hind leg, then the wires around his hips, I continued, "You know most of my neighbors would kill you right now, on the spot. I think they simply misunderstand you. I know that some coyotes prey upon the local sheep simply for sport. I will have none of that here. So, I would like to make a deal with you. If I cut you out of this fence I ask that you and your family do not kill my lambs."

We reached an agreement and I cut him all the way out of the fence. The last wire to be cut was right around his muzzle. This was the scariest part for him and me. I re-iterated my care, snipped the wire, and down to the ground he leapt. As he trotted off, he would look back at me and I would remind him of our deal. I thanked him for trusting me to take care of him.

Wild animals assert safety versus danger in split seconds. They instantly determine whether they trust, are not sure, or distrust the situation. Any doubt and they are usually off in another direction. It always amazes me how much actually gets communicated through the silent airwaves of telepathy. I started to think about how people ascertain trust. People have similar instincts to our animal brothers and yet we tend not to listen with the same fervor. We may make split second decisions about others; the problem is we are not often aware of our decisions.

We learned in our early years not to honor our animal senses. Sometimes we just don't like someone we just met. We generally don't respect our first response, and counter our feelings by doubting ourselves. We go out of our way to prove that our initial feelings about this person are unreliable. Our rational mind quickly takes over with an assessment that we are just being paranoid or unkind. In an effort to ignore our own discomfort, we befriend this person only to find at some future date they betray us. In hindsight we say, "I knew I didn't like that person."

Other times we meet a new person at a party or a conference and we feel naturally fond towards them. It feels like we could talk to them for hours. It's easy to be with them and our curiosity towards them is spontaneous. In this case, a high level of trust is felt between the two individuals and they often become life long friends.

More often we meet someone at a party and feel neutral about them. They seem nice enough but we feel a need to get to know them better. We need more time to understand them and build trust with them. In these situations, trust must be developed over time. Trust in others is further developed, person by person, through time and experience. If trust is broken it takes tremendous commitment and recurrent demonstration for trust to be rebuilt.

Without trust various dysfunctions in communication and coordination occur. For a team that lacks trust within the individuals, a group of competitive individuals results. Projected results may get accomplished, but a sense of belonging and deeper contribution never gets developed. A hyper vigilance and personal withholding reduces personal contentment and creates an uncompassionate environment.

Horses don't ignore their sensate experience. As animals they gauge trust, not by words spoken, but by how they feel. Trust with others is developed over time. We can chase a wild horse in a round pen and bring it to submission in half an hour. This doesn't mean that we've gained the horse's trust. We just tired him out. The horse learns to trust the human gradually, each point of contact building on the previous session. Training a reliable horse takes recurrent reinforcement that we are not dangerous, that we are competent socially and that we respect his need to be a contributing member of the team. It only takes a minute to break trust, but it can take a thousand hours to repair it.

Horses gauge trust from an intuitive rather than intellectual perspective. Their trust barometer is measured by their feelings of safety versus danger. When they feel mentally, physically and spiritually safe their body is relaxed and they trust their surroundings. When they don't feel safe, their body tenses and their distrust is reflected as mental or physical resistance.

It is easy to see when a horse distrusts his situation. He is tense, stiff, agitated, irritated. He does not know how to lie. Humans, on the other hand, can say one thing with their body and something entirely different with their mouth. Somewhere along the line we learned how to tolerate this *inauthenticity* as a species. This strange ability to be mentally and physically incongruent seems to be unique to humans.

For some reason we have allowed this trait to go unattended for so long that we have a lot of ground to cover to relearn how to trust ourselves and other humans. Because we can *talk* our way around how we are feeling we can end up lying to ourselves and to those around us, whereas a horse can only show what he's feeling.

Trust is fundamental in any relational context. As soon as an animal or human enters a new relationship or situation, our animal senses are assessing the authenticity of others. When trust is not present, coordination and communication break down. Backbiting, sabotage, avoidance, resentful employees, defensive managers and gossip are just a few of the negative consequences. Trust is an emotional skill that we create, build, maintain, and sustain.

The issue of trust, at first invisible, is actually one of the primary sources of either the success or deterioration of relationships. Trust can be broken in many ways. I like to break the issue of trust down into three categories: sincerity, competency and reliability. And then further by domains. Drilling down the specific area that trust is broken within a team allows the team to develop new strategies for rebuilding trust that has been broken.

Linda Kohanov, in *The Tao of Equus*, wrote about her experiences working in equine facilitated psychotherapy. Speaking on authenticity and trust, she explains:

> *"The men and women I counsel have a terrible time admitting their true feelings to themselves, let alone to others, because they've been taught to disregard their emotions by the authority figures in their lives. They're caught in this vicious circle of feeling confused and threatened around incongruent people, yet not being able to act congruently themselves. Horses are able to break this cycle by showing people what they are feeling without sugarcoating it, yet somehow it's not so threatening when these animals see through you.*

I think it's because horses don't have any ulterior motives. They're just responding honestly in the moment. The ability to lie to oneself and to others is prominent in post conquest consciousness. While animals will occasionally fake injury to draw a predator away from their young, their ability to deceive is limited by one important reason: they can't speak. Lies are almost exclusively based in language."

When we don't trust others, we contract away from social engagement. We respond to the energetic congruence or incongruence of others just like horses do. We may not realize that we are in a state of distrust, but we may feel irritated or self-conscious. Underneath this contraction lies the barometer of trust. Horses don't doubt their sensate information. To illustrate this point let me tell you a little story.

THE LOSS OF EXCELLENCE

In early 2002 I was hired by a consultant to work with a team of senior VPs of a Fortune 500 company. The consultant was in a confidential coaching relationship with the team leader and had no prior experience with the rest of the team. The team leader and the consultant had organized a two-day event with the goal of encouraging his staff to become more accountable for their roles. But in an act of incongruence, they asked the team to come for two days of their own learning in leadership. It was sold to them as something for their own development, which I unfortunately found out mid-way through the program.

During the first half hour of introductions, I read the body language of the team and saw that they had no respect for their team leader. Their arms were folded at their chests and they sat back in their chairs. They looked skeptical with a façade of openness. The team leader had an agenda for his team that he had not disclosed and they were already feeling his inauthenticity at a deep subconscious level. His inner goal of wanting them to be more accountable did not match his outer story of altruistic encouragement. I don't think the team even realized that they did not trust their leader. It was not in their schema of awareness to pay attention to what was not spoken.

As we got rolling it became clear; not only did they not trust their leader, the team had no organizing principle. These team members were all highly qualified, intelligent people. Without an organizing principle, they had each created their own plan and were all off doing what they thought they should be doing.

As we began to work with the horses, it became clear that they all demonstrated the same style of leadership. They were lone rangers, circling off to work hard, over-efforting and seeing each other more as competitors than partners. When faced with this visual demonstration, they each muttered that what was being reflected was the result of the founder's tyrannical style. They were resigned about changing their internal culture. They acknowledged that they were encouraged to be creative, but were consistently squashed whenever they attempted to present new ideas. When resignation is present, everything seems hopeless— Why bother?

The way each department leader compensated for this lack of support was to go off on their own and do their own thing. This, in turn, created a top-level (not necessarily top performing) team that had no organizing principle for being together because they had never figured out how to think in a collective way.

By the end of the day, the horse activities had begun to open the stream of conversation. They were beginning to think together and resolve the gaps in their assumptions about what needed to be done, which, in my opinion, was a good thing. The team was beginning to talk about their breakdowns and how they felt resigned about discussing them. The conversation was quickly closed down (against my recommendation) by the leader and consultant, and their agenda started to leak into the room.

I had a sense that we were at a significant juncture. The team leader felt the constraint of time and decided he would rather push through the material than have his team discuss their opinions and feelings. By the next morning the team was in full resistance. Trust was broken. They voiced their resentment that they had been told that this was an opportunity for their own development only to realize that the leader had another agenda. They felt lied to.

The team leader, once again, decided to push through his agenda, rather than dealing with the breakdown. We worked with the horses again. One of the department leaders dug in his heals and his resistant mood wafted over the group. This man I will call Tom was caught in his own internal dialogue that he was not good enough. He felt that he had been set up and that there was no opportunity to be heard.

Internally he felt embarrassed that he had shown himself to the group because he did not trust how they would respond to his vulnerability. With the lack of trust in the group not being addressed, he turned the uncomfortable feelings onto himself, thinking maybe he was defective. Several of Tom's teammates began to feel protective of Tom. They were not going to abandon him, and so they basically spoke to the group that they did not like the process.

The team was no longer open to repairing the trust that had been broken because they felt like there was no room for their feelings and opinions to be acknowledged. Without allowing the team to process their feelings of distrust, and go into the murky waters, redemption remained a stone's throw away.

This story illustrates a leader whose team didn't trust him. Their bodies and their actions revealed their resistance. The opportunity to have a well-coordinated team who supported each other was lost. Things still got done, but people did not feel good about their work or their team. They went along begrudgingly and with a lack of inspiration. They felt used as opposed to included. This particular leader missed his opportunity to develop his leaders into thriving, fully engaged participants. He still got them to perform, but just enough to get the job done. The potential talent on the team remained below the surface, frustrated and unencouraged.

AUTHENTICITY

Unlike human beings, horses don't judge or reject us for
what we're feeling; it's the act of trying to suppress our
emotions that drives them insane.

—Linda Kohanov

The horse's willingness to trust the human arises out of its keen ability to perceive the human's authenticity, silently measuring the coherence between inner thoughts and outer expression. The horse perceives what is *actually* happening inside the human and mirrors this internal reality. The horse does not listen to our words, our convincing tone or smiling face. It listens only to that part of us that is authentic, that is naturally inside of us at that moment. If we are afraid and pretend not to be, with a smile on our face, the horse will respond only to our fear, often getting afraid himself. When a horse becomes afraid it gets anxious, jumpy and often dangerous. If we are angry or terse inside and act congenial on the outside, the horse will get irritated and may pin its ears and threaten to kick or bite.

Because horses are so sensitive to our *inner animal,* it becomes paramount for our physical safety to be aware of our internal reality at all times when handling horses. Horses can teach us how to respect our inner feelings without blame and judgment. They can teach us how to be honest because they consistently point out our incompetence at being truly honest. They demand our authenticity. When we are inauthentic with the horse, problems become apparent immediately. The following stories illustrate how sensitive horses are to our inner thoughts and fears.

KEEPING SECRETS

In the spring of 2001 I was introduced to Barbara Rector, one of the pioneers of Equine Facilitated Psychotherapy (EFP) and co-founder of EFMHA (Equine Facilitated Mental Health Association). She was holding a clinic at a friend's house. One of the participants I shall call Patty went out to the center of the arena to work with a 17-hand warmblood gelding named Johann. Barbara asked Patty to follow Johann's lead and for her to listen to what he had to reveal to her. After about three minutes, Johann started yawning. He yawned several times, each time stretching his head low to the ground, rolling his eyes and opening his mouth wide. This display was very unusual. It wasn't like a yawn of boredom or satisfaction at finishing a job.

As my curiosity increased I realized he was portraying a gagging or choking motion, as if something was stuck in his throat. I knew nothing was actually wrong with him, so I wondered if he was trying to say something to Patty. Somatically, he was representing energy stuck in her throat.

He yawned again and rolled his eyes. His mouth open, WIDE OPEN, at Patty's eye level. She was watching him closely as he lowered his head to smell the ground at her feet. As he lifted his head again, he stretched his neck out and yawned. His gestures were getting more earnest and exaggerated. Barbara intercepted and asked Patty, "What message do you think Johann is giving you?"

The blood seemed to drain from Patty's face as her cheeks paled. Barbara quietly suggested to Patty that she mimic Johann's neck stretching yawns. As she made this motion she looked just like Johann did a few moments ago: leaning forward and stretching her throat and opening her mouth as if to yawn. Without realizing it, her movements provided her with a somatic release of the energy that had been blocked in her throat. Barbara asked Patty, "How are you feeling now?" She shook her head in disbelief as tears welled in her eyes.

"I've been keeping a secret and I am afraid to tell the truth."

As if he understood her words, Johann relaxed for the first time since he had been with Patty. He licked his lips as if to encourage her to become authentic with her inner dilemma.

As she debriefed her experience she confessed that she felt out of integrity with her staff at the handicapped riding program she operated.

The previous summer she had been on a trail ride after work and had fallen off her horse and injured her back. After the accident she had become intensely afraid of horses, and she had been paralyzed by fear of telling her staff. She had become conflicted about offering her riding program if she herself was afraid of horses. Even though she had other instructors teaching her students, she was still concerned that she had failed her program in some way. She was deeply afraid that if she told the truth that her world would come tumbling down and everything she had built would be destroyed.

Johann's expressive yawning mirrored Patty's incongruence between her inner fear and her outer expression of confidence. His need to yawn over and over again was an unspoken urge to release the energetic block in her throat so that she could bring voice to her inner dialogue. While she had been presenting herself to the human group as a professional, competent person, inside she felt like a liar and was afraid that someone would find out about her fear of horses. Johann in his usual equine style was sending signals about something *stuck in the throat*. His actions created a place for Patty to become authentic and honest.

Most of the participants in the class had been around this work enough to accept that what may appear to a newcomer as pure coincidence is actually synchronous harmony; *harmony* being the resolution of conflict. Barbara respected Johann's gestures and encouraged Patty to repeat the gestures herself. By leaning forward and yawning like Johann, she somatically released the block in her throat that had been literally holding her secret.

Group process and one-on-one counseling had not created an

opening for Patty to realize how much her fear had gripped her into isolation. The mystery of Johann's ability to feel the conflict inside of Patty becomes his gift of healing. His persistence in announcing her *blocked throat* acted as cues to Barbara to work through Patty's body as opposed to her intellect. Her thoughtful mind had already buried the secret and developed a well-defended method of denial.

Patty could not deny Johann's message by pretending to be confident. She knew that his yawn was unique to her. However, she didn't know how to come out into the open with her secret. Once Johann had called her attention to the matter, it was up to Patty to move into the same energetic, intuitive landscape that Johann lived and breathed in. It was up to her to pick up the insights in his actions. Once Patty acknowledged her fear, she was able to move into action with it rather than pretending she was fine. As she voiced her fears she realized that they were actually ungrounded.

Patty finally had words to express her fears and release her secret. Post session she agreed to go home and discuss her dilemma with her business partners. She reported later that they were very understanding, and relieved to have her honest reflection about what was going on for her internally. Now they could work together to resolve the issues that Patty had privately been concerned about. They were supportive and offered to help her regain her confidence around horses. They did not abandon her, as she had feared.

THE BODY REMEMBERS

Jim was a successful doctor in the San Francisco Bay Area. He was a sweet and quiet man. Soft spoken and consistent, he seemed like he couldn't hurt a flea. As he started to lunge Stella, she became irritated and began bucking and even kicked out at me. I was shocked. I had never seen her act this way before.

Stella was the most docile horse I had ever known and this

display of violence was a complete shift away from her friendly demeanor. In the four years I had owned her, I had never seen her show any sign of aggression. Clearly she was sensing something that wasn't readily available to us. I immediately asked him to stop. I went between him and Stella to reassure her that I was there and she could trust me.

I could tell she was reflecting something about his inner feelings that wasn't being addressed. I intuitively took the lunge whip away from Jim even though he had not used it in any way (the whip was only a reminder to keep a good distance from the horse when on the long line, not to be used on the horse).

I wanted to slow things down so I asked Jim to walk Stella quietly in hand from a centered and balanced presence. Within minutes he had her walking and trotting quietly. During his debrief, he shared with the group that when he was a boy he was beaten for his horse's mistakes. As a child he rode his horse to school and to do family chores. When he fell off on the trail and his horse came home without him, his grandfather would beat him with a whip. Holding the lunge whip brought back his body's memory of fear and anger.

Now I could understand why Stella went crazy. She felt his unresolved anxiety even though he was not cognitively aware of it himself. By dropping the whip and walking the horse quietly, he was able to be with the horse on new ground. He wrote later to say that his work with Stella had allowed him to be with horses in a new way. He no longer blamed them for his former punishment and actually found a fondness for them that he had forgotten.

Jim exemplifies a situation in which the body holds the memory of an intense historical experience. Just holding the lunge whip in his hand brought back to life some long-buried insult that his muscles still remembered. How did Stella feel his anxiety so accurately? The experience with Jim and Stella was a wake-up call for me to look even deeper than I had been looking. I was beginning to understand that if someone had unresolved anger or rage still living in their body, they might actually be putting themselves in danger around the horse if they were not acknowledging the deeper residual energy that was being transmitted to the horse.

In other words, a person can be inauthentic and not even be conscious of being inauthentic. Inauthenticity can be pre-cognitive. It can be the incongruence between bodily experience and mental awareness. Or it can be an incongruence between mental stories and spiritual longing. One thing is certain; when inauthenticity is present the horses become aggressive. The lie that results from being inauthentic is literally not safe for a horse to be around.

When Jim was holding the whip and his body was re-living the beatings his body language was not matching the words coming out of his mouth. When I took the whip away from him, his body relaxed and came back into an authentic expression of the story he was saying out loud.

This case study reminds me of a story I read in an article on fear. In the late 1800s several physicians conducted a study on fear and the brain. They were trying to isolate the part of the brain that triggers a fear response. One patient we will call Samantha had suffered a dramatic injury that left her with no short-term memory—she could not remember events from one moment to the next. So each day when she arrived at the doctor's office, she would shake the doctor's hand and introduce herself. Months into treatment, the doctor put a pin in his hand and when she went to shake his hand in greeting, she was pricked by the pin. The pain from the prick caused her to back up a step.

The next day when she arrived at the doctor's office, she introduced herself as usual but was unwilling to shake his hand. She could not remember why she would not shake his hand, but she refused nonetheless. This simple story illustrates clearly how the memory of pain or trauma lives in the body despite our mind's attempts to resolve the angst.

I'M OK, NO I'M NOT

The minute Jane came into the round pen, Mimi, a petite white mare, became agitated. Her quiet and sweet nature turned into a mass of anxiety. She began pushing against Jane aggressively, trying to toss her off balance. I moved in between Mimi and Jane—creating some distance between them. Mimi, still agitated, rubbed her neck on the fence like she was trying to rub off a burr embedded in her skin and she paced back and forth nervously. I stepped Mimi away from Jane several more feet and she began to calm down.

"So, talk to me," I said.

Jane replied, "I don't know what is going on."

"Mimi is responding to an unacknowledged, intense energy and feels a need to get rid of it. If she is responding to something inside of you—perhaps some unacknowledged energy—what do you think she is reflecting about you?" I asked.

"I don't know. It can't be what I think it is." She muttered as tears began to stream down her face. She tried to hold her breath to no avail. And as her body demanded air, she finally screamed in a raw guttural voice, "I am terrified that my husband is going to leave me! My first husband left the children and me. I was devastated and I can't get over this fear that it is going to happen to me again."

"Has your current husband threatened to leave you?"

"No, he is wonderful. I don't know why I am so afraid." Jane wept. "I am so angry. Do you think that is why Mimi is so upset?"

"Yes, Jane, she could be mirroring your internal angst and unresolved anger about your original loss," I gently suggested.

A few moments passed and I drew her attention back to the horse, "Notice that since you have become more authentic, and you have acknowledged your inner thoughts, Mimi has settled down."

Mimi's dramatic response to Jane facilitated Jane's acceptance of this intense residual fear. It was no longer O.K. to keep it buried inside and pretend she was fine. She needed to deal with her past and look into the present to determine if history would repeat itself or if she was being driven by the fear of abandonment that her physical body still held as a *true story*. She further realized that if she did not become responsible for her fear and anxiety she could very well create a self-fulfilling prophecy of rejection.

Jane had been able to fool herself and her therapist into believing that she had healed from being abandoned by her first husband. The horse, however, felt the unresolved trauma. If the horse could feel her inauthenticity, she realized that her children probably also felt it. She decided to continue working on this new insight so that her children would not have to take on her inner emotional state like Mimi had done.

Authenticity is expressed by a *genuine wholeness* between the inner and outer emotional, energetic states of being. Patty and Jane's experience with the horses revealed that their inner emotional state did not match their outer emotional expression. Their internal and external stories were in conflict. In Jim's case, his internal physical experience was different than his outer expression of confidence and presence. Jim had resolved his childhood dilemmas intellectually, but his body had not resolved the trauma.

In each situation, the horse had a strong reaction to this incongruence. Horses are unwilling to accept our false pretense. They only listen to what is on the inside. When our inner and outer presentation is incongruent, the horse enters a heightened state of agitation.

Do we humans feel this kind of incongruity the way that Mimi and Stella did? *What do we do with this sensory information?* Sometimes we just don't trust somebody. Why? Perhaps we are as sensitive as the horse, but we negate it. We question ourselves instead of giving ourselves permission to just not feel right about something.

We take responsibility for something that is not ours to take. Horses don't take it in. Just like other wild animals, they do not hold in negative or excess energy. They discharge it. When they are uncomfortable with a person's negative or excess energy, they express it by fleeing the scene, running frantically, whinnying, bucking, pinning their ears back, yawning, shaking their head, defecating, or even rolling. They shake it off—they don't take it *into* themselves.

Wouldn't it be great if we could learn how to shake off that excess energy rather than hold it in our muscles until it becomes embodied, chronic fear?

Horses that are confined to daily life in a stall sometimes do not physically have the room to dissipate the excess energy they are feeling. Like people who confine themselves to their cubicle at work, they hold in the excess energy. Energy has to go somewhere. It doesn't just disappear. Chronically held energy leads to constriction of the life force, which in turn leads to emotional, physical, or spiritual distress.

Horses that are further confined *emotionally* by their owners, (much like people who are confined emotionally), begin to display various behavior problems including bad attitudes, resistance, resentment, nipping, ear pinning, tail swishing, and a general lackluster appearance or soulless eyes.

Horses know how to be responsible for themselves. When they are not allowed this basic privilege, they suffer within the confines of the human's projection. When a horse reacts to a person who is being inauthentic it is as though they are offended that this person is not being responsible for himself or herself. Being a social animal that knows—with every ounce of its body—that the survivability of the whole depends on each individual's capacity to be self-responsible, the horse is irritated by the inauthentic human's lack of self-responsibility.

Even though we cannot say for sure what the horse is thinking, we can assume that the horse is *declaring a breakdown*. He is not trusting and rather than just fleeing the situation, becomes increasingly aggressive toward the perpetrator. I often wonder if the dramatic displays of aggression in these situations are the horse's attempt to shout out, *"Don't lie to me. It's not safe!"*

Over the years I have experienced far more aggressive

reflections of in-authenticity in group situations and private sessions. I have learned to sense the energy of individuals in a learning group. If I begin to feel agitated, or tense, I am on the alert for in-authenticity. It is necessary for me to be hyper-alert, because I don't want to risk either the people or the horses' well being—physical, emotional or spiritual—by putting that person in the round pen with the horse.

I have even had horses begin to race around the arena for no apparent reason when a new group arrives and no one is even in the arena with them. Sure enough, there is a person in the group who is not being self-responsible. Their intense response to someone who, at times, can be over fifty feet away is quite astounding and *commands respect*. In these situations I address the issue before the person is allowed to approach the horse.

CONFIDENCE

Small wonder that confidence languishes, for it thrives
only on honesty, on honor, on the sacredness of
obligations, on faithful protection, on unselfish
performance. Without them it cannot live.
—*Franklin D. Roosevelt*

We don't find confidence. Confidence finds us. We cannot run after confidence, wish it or desire it. It finds us when we are applying ourselves gracefully to something outside of ourselves. It arises out of an unabashed focus on our goals. Confidence is not a 'mind' game; it is a 'being' game, a practice in *mindlessness*.

Confidence arises out of a deep-seated belief in ourselves and what we care about. When we are confident about ourselves we're not in a self-sabotaging story or negative self-assessment about our ability to manifest our dreams. Confidence, in its simplest form, is simply a state of being in which we are not being self-conscious. We are not worrying about how we are doing or what others think of us.

People and horses are inspired by a person who embodies confidence because there is an unspoken sense that they are *sure of* themselves. They are focused on their goals and their ability to take care of themselves. Their personal boundaries are clear—allowing others to know how to interact easily with them.

Martin Luther King is a great example of a man who knew what he stood for without question or shame. His conviction to his beliefs was so strong that other people had no option but to choose to agree with him or not. There was no fuzzy ground. He did not say, "I have a dream?" He said, " I have a *dream*!!"

In our self-leadership practice with horses, the horse reflects back to us the importance of embodiment. They expect us to believe in our goals and embody the commitment required to attain them. When these elements are missing, the horse quickly loses interest in being part of our team. Without clarity of purpose and a *commitment to follow through*, the horse becomes a thousand-pound hunk of flesh that is immovable by even the strongest individual.

It is as if the horse is asking, "Can I rely on you to know what to do if danger is present?" If they don't feel our confidence, they *know* they cannot depend on us. If we consistently lack confidence around them, they begin to lose respect for us—they're certain that we do not know how to defend ourselves and therefore cannot participate in protecting the herd from danger. They begin to look for ways to avoid us, move around us, or push us away altogether.

Confidence is not so much about having competency—though competency contributes to feeling assured of our ability to produce results. I have seen confidence present without competence. When learning new skills or developing confidence in new domains, we can cross appropriate the sense of confidence we have in other areas and apply it to the learning environment we are currently in.

CROSS-APPROPRIATING CONFIDENCE

John was an architect in his mid-fifties. He was attending a Leadership and Horses™ seminar to develop his ability to expand his business. He had never worked with horses before, but he was open and curious about how working with them might help him in his professional life. He was the last person to work with Lottie that day. Lottie had gradually become slower and less engaged with her human students, since many of the previous participants had lacked confidence in their commitment to their goals. I was concerned that she had quit for the day and that the other participants would not get a chance to see her come to life in the presence of confidence and intention.

No sooner had John taken his place in the center of the circle than Lottie sprang to life with a bold and lively trot. He held a centered, focused presence, which gave Lottie the message that he believed in himself and his goal. His confidence gave her confidence. They looked like a united pair performing eloquently together as if they had been doing this all of their lives.

The equestrians in the group were immediately envious of his apparent competency at awakening Lottie out of her disinterest. They wondered how he could be so successful if he had never lunged a horse before. They had also become re-energized by the fluidity of communication possible between man and horse. They were inspired by his presence and clarity.

During the debrief, John revealed that he had been a professional football player in his earlier years. When he was working with the bay and white mare, he was reminded of the presence required to work with the football team and the opposing players. He remembered what his body felt like when he was engaged in close-contact negotiation. He imagined he was *that body* as he worked with Lottie.

He illustrated, quite simply, the example of cross-appropriating his competency from one domain into a new domain of learning. His success in embodying the confidence he felt when playing football opened a whole new way for him to approach his business clients with the same confidence. He found that his clients were just as moved by his newfound confidence as Lottie had been.

THE POWER OF "CENTER"

Plutarch, an early philosopher of leadership, found that all of the great leaders he studied had a *sense of destiny* about them.

In the early 1900's another philosopher by the name of Napoleon Hill concluded that the great leaders of his day had a sense of their *mission in life*.

In 1989, two professors of the Stanford Business School, Dr. James Collins and Dr. Jerry Porras, analyzed over one-hundred successful executives and concluded that each one had a sense of purpose, mission and vision.[3] These leaders had a *well-defined center*—a core purpose. These ingredients allow a person to find that inner confidence that they can learn to settle into.

When we are confident, we feel *on purpose*. We are connected to what is important to us. We are focused on the results we are committed to producing and do not get swept into the emotional drama of the dilemmas we may face. Rather than being in reaction, we are aware that we can *choose* how to respond. We are open to possibility and our imagination is present and available. Our internal judge is not chattering away with its constrictive attitude.

We are not threatened by other people's opinions because we are sure of our own stand. The diagram below reflects the ingredients of confidence.

RELATION TO	QUALITY
Self	Know yourself Know what you are good at and what you are not good at
Other	Curious about what you do not know Open to other points of view
World	Know what you care about Focused on the bigger picture or purpose

When we are centered we are *present* to our mental frame of mind, our physical state of awareness, our emotional tone and our spiritual longing. In relationship to others, we are *open* to different interpretations and points of view. For example, someone may be giving us a strong assessment and yet we are able to stay flexible— remembering that it is just his or her *point of view* at that moment. Their assessment may be grounded and they may have a good point. On the other hand they may be reactive and off-center. We maintain our own center, *what we care about*, in relationship to them.

When we are centered we are connected to the bigger picture, our *for the sake of what*. "For the sake of what" are we having conversations with others, taking actions and investing ourselves? We literally have a "center" that we are organized around, physically, spiritually, and mentally.

When we are off-center, we are triggered into automatic responses and emotional reactions to life and its inherent dilemmas. We lose sight of the big picture. We get caught in our head, gripped in old stories or moral judgment. We look to justify our reactiveness in either collapsing into self-judgment and/or making others wrong so we can feel right.

Corresponding emotional states include anxiety, irritation, anger, depression, resentment or frustration. Our physical body may experience heat, shortness of breath, fixed eyes, rigid muscles, or a tight throat. When we are in reaction, our mood is off, and conflicts tend to get accelerated or intensified rather than being resolved.

Towards others we reflect resistance and inflexibility. Our relationship to the world or herd is disorganized and lacks focus. We have forgotten that we have an important role to play in relation to our herd. We feel alone and isolated.

Falling into fear, distrust or judgment, throws us off-center, away from choice. We begin to focus our attention on what is wrong with our circumstance or us. In this state of reaction, we tend to create negative self-assessments about ourselves. We unknowingly create our own confinement and end up walking around our life *small and afraid*.

The diagram below summarizes the difference between being centered and being off-center.

RELATION TO	CENTER	OFF-CENTER
Self	Present	Triggered
Other	Open	Judgmental
World	Connected	Disorganized

Richard Strozzi Heckler, Ph.D., a pioneer in the field of Somatics, writes in his book *Anatomy of Change*:

> *"Center is the starting place in the continuum of moving through change. Center is like the eyepiece of the telescope: it establishes a focus and place of departure for the entire spectrum of learning....*
>
> *It is not that we have to find our center and then maintain it at all costs. Center is more of a reference point to return to, so we can relate to our life situations in a complete way. When Morihei Uyeshiba, the founder of aikido, was asked if he ever lost his balance, he replied, "Yes, all the time, but I regain it so fast that you do not see me lose it."*
>
> *This 'state of center' is a doorway, a place to begin feeling our deeper urges, our possibilities in the world, and the expansiveness of our excitement."*

PLAYING SMALL

Mary was a very successful CFO at a telecom firm in Silicon Valley. In our private sessions, she revealed her preoccupation with negative self-assessments. She thought she was ugly, fat and that she wasn't good with people. I saw a very different picture. She had a beautiful chiseled face and an angelic quality of presence. Her whole beingness made me want to be close to her. I knew from having watched her in several of our courses that she was well liked and others spoke highly of her.

I asked her if other people had given her the same assessments that she had of herself. She answered, "Quite the contrary." The difference between her actual identity in the world and her self-perception was incoherent.

During our work together she began to see that her negative self-perceptions were no longer useful to her and were actually undermining her progress in life. She also knew that just deciding not to have negative feelings towards herself was not enough to produce a significant change.

I suggested a new practice of choosing three people whom she trusted to ask their assessments of her in specific areas. Her task was to pay more attention to their assessments rather than to her own negative self-assessments. This helped, but she would still allow her negative cheerleader to get the best of her. Talking around her issues was not getting us anywhere. It was time to work with the horses and get their feedback.

We went out to work with Sadie. Mary was surprised how well she worked the mare and quickly started apologizing for her success as if it was purely an accident. I offered her a different interpretation that Sadie was reflecting her focused presence and enjoyed partnering with her. While she demonstrated a lack of self-consciousness in the arena, her post performance assessment of her success did not match. She was not noticing when she was moving in the world with confidence even though others did.

The mare's visual display of engagement in her leadership still surprised her. Her recurrent success as reflected through Sadie's graceful and engaged movement began to feel good to her. Her body relaxed and a smile crossed her face. She felt good. She rewarded Sadie and the bay mare responded with even more beauty of movement.

She learned that by denying her success in the arena, she was also denying Sadie's success. Her interest in the horse feeling successful helped her to pave a new path towards self-acceptance. Her capacity to care for another was the very ground from which she could learn to care for herself. She saw that by negating herself and not acknowledging her own dignity, she was consequently letting others down. The horse was a visual example of *those others* in her life. While it seemed paradoxical, she realized that the way to take care of their dignity was to acknowledge her own strengths and successes.

Once she saw that a positive self-image was more important to others than even to herself, her commitment to change her story was exponentially deeper. She also realized that by not accepting positive, affirming assessments from others, she was ultimately disrespecting them.

The practice of believing others' positive feelings towards her was fundamental in shifting her self-perception and allowed her to find a new peace that created a balance in her life that she had longed for.

TAKING A STAND

Behind all leadership, especially *leadership of the self*, something is at stake. What we care about throughout our life changes. For some, what we care about is having children; for others it is about getting a career promotion; or saving the planet; healing others.

Sometimes we lose sight of what we care about. We get distracted by our long *to-do list* or simply being busy. Some leaders think being busy means achieving results. Accomplishing tasks alone does not make one a leader. Sometimes the activities we spend so much time focusing on are actually detracting us from our deeper goals and ambitions. We may resist our inner ambitions because of subconscious stories that those ambitions are not worthy enough. Life happens to us. We are at the affect of our circumstance. Our spiritual self may begin to feel powerless and ungrounded, and yet we continue to busy ourselves with mental chores.

Horses can sense when we no longer know what we care about. When we don't know what we care about, the horse has no direction to follow. There is no action—no possibility to move towards. When we don't know what we care about anymore, the authentic conversation is to *re-find* it. The practice becomes reawakening the inner passion for life; the spirit's calling.

SHOW ME THE GATE

Beth was a mother, housewife and real estate broker. She was in a phase in her life in which she felt like she was wandering. She felt fragile. She often looked at the ground while talking to her group.

She had witnessed several participants come into the round pen and discuss their goals and intentions and receive reflections and insights from the horse guide, Angel, a chestnut mare of medium size.

It was her turn to speak about her own ambitions and ask Angel to walk with her on her leadership path. As she began speaking she lowered her head, looked at the ground and slacked her shoulders. Her voice was soft and flat. Angel lowered her head as if she too was looking at the ground as listened to Beth speak. The practice in the arena was to declare a goal that she would then practice her leadership with Angel. Instead, Beth asked the horse, "What do *you* think I should do?"

Beth's habit was to be appeasing. Her posture was flaccid, her energy withdrawn disappearing into the ground. I wondered if her request of Angel to define her goals mirrored a habit of giving others the power to make decisions for her. After Beth asked Angel several times what to do, Angel picked her head up and nudged Beth as if to say, "Follow me."

Beth followed Angel, who without hesitation walked her straight to the designated exit gate of the round pen. Her group sighed, as she looked at the gate puzzled.

A woman in her group called out, "She just walked you to the gate."

Her group collectively whispered, "Oh, my God..."

"What?" I asked. One woman spoke, "She was just fired from her job last week before she came here. Her boss literally showed her the gate."

A silence settled among the group of fourteen women who were part of Beth's learning team. They were astounded by Angel's direct and psychic feedback.

Angel reflected for Beth that if she did not know what she cared about and insisted on looking to others to provide her with direction that it was quite likely they would ask her to leave the arena. In follow-up sessions, Beth was able to realize that she was not making decisions for herself and that it was producing confusion and disinterest in others.

The people in her life were tired of her lack of self-leadership and had started to avoid her. They sensed that she was not *at home in her own skin*. Beth's *unconfidence* made them uncomfortable being around her. They were relieved that Angel was able to get a message to Beth so that they could all support her in finding *her* "stand"—a self-knowledge; self-acceptance; and the consequent extension of that uniqueness outwards to others and to the world.

Knowing what we *really* care about is not easy. It takes a deep questing for our *purpose in life*: our calling. The books *Repacking your Bags* and *The Power of Purpose* (by Leider and Shapiro) are excellent resources for this inquiry.

"Taking a stand" is a declaration of all of who we *are* and who we are *becoming*. It encompasses our values and ethics about living a good life, about making a contribution, about relationship and family. It means acting with rigor and intention, without apology. It requires the courage to accept that not everyone will follow.

Courage follows the unabashed forward movement that our confidence demonstrates. Courage itself comes out of being in touch with our stand and being willing to take the risk of standing apart from others in order to be truly who we are supposed to be.

When we are unconfident about how others will relate to our ideas, we are not taking a stand for what matters to us. We are allowing old stories to inhibit our progress, consciously or unconsciously. When we put aside self-consciousness, our vision of new possibilities can flourish. New stories of the future become tangible. Allowing our imagination to inform our quest brings a natural confidence forward. Suspending the judge encourages us to be truly ourselves without embarrassment. Sharing our love without ego, (as exemplified by Mother Theresa), bypasses the enemies of confidence.

SUSPENDING THE JUDGE

Kimberly was a new mom and career executive at AT&T. She

came to the ranch to work on her self-confidence. She confessed that she shied away from more responsibility at work. She thought that if she could feel more confident, she would be able to take more risks and accept her boss's attempts to promote her. She thought that she could talk herself into being more confident.

As we began to brush Sadie, the big red mare pinned her ears back in a show of aggression. This was extremely unusual and important to address before we continued being around the horse. I asked Kimberly, "What is happening for you now? How do you feel?"

She replied, "I feel fine."

I explained Sadie's show of aggression could be a reflection of a negative voice she was expressing internally. Kimberly looked confused. I asked her, "What is the tone of Sadie's energy right now?"

"She seems angry," replied Kimberly.

"If Sadie is mirroring your energy, do you resonate with feeling angry?"

Softly and convincingly she replied, "Oh, no. I always put on a good face."

She began to brush Sadie again, hoping to ward off the conversation. Sadie pinned her ears again and became more agitated. Again I stopped Kimberly and asked her how she was feeling. At first she wasn't sure. I knew there was some reason for Sadie's anger, but I was hoping that Kimberly would find her own revelation.

"It's very important, if we are to respect Sadie, that we try to figure out why she is so irritated."

Kimberly looked down at the ground, thinking. And then she lifted her face in a big "aha!"

"I get angry with myself all the time. I get mean with myself; sometimes I even tear at my hair. I hate myself. I think I should be better, I can't stop feeling bad about myself."

Now it made sense why Sadie had acted aggressively. I knew Sadie had seen something in Kimberly. It really shocked Kimberly to be revealed in such a dramatic way. She confessed that she recognized herself in Sadie's mirror of her own rage.

I asked her, "Can you see the power your internal mood has on the others in your life, including Sadie?"

"My kids" she mumbled, "Wow, if Sadie is feeling my self-hate, I worry that my kids do too."

Once she realized her beloved children were at stake, she became very committed to change. We continued brushing Sadie. The horse was now relaxed and quiet, as if just bringing this energy into the external conversation was enough for her to feel safe and enjoy the grooming ritual.

While Kimberly had come to work on her confidence (so she could be better at work), her point of focus became how she was as a mother. Her children were far more important to her than a job title. She realized that her family was *enough* to care about. She didn't have to focus on her career path as much as she had assumed. She had bought the cultural push to *be more*, as if that, in and of itself, would make her a better person—someone she could feel confident about.

Through Sadie's assistance in revealing what it felt like to others when Kimberly was being internally critical, we were able to develop a set of practices to decline her inner critic and integrate a healthier self-image into her private emotional life. She became more observant about how her inner thoughts may be affecting those around her. Her path towards self-confidence was not what she had expected. She began to notice that when she wasn't thinking about *how she* was doing, she actually felt successful. Over time she began to feel a sense of peace and satisfaction in being aware of her own senses. When she noticed she was beginning to nip at herself, she would go outside and take a walk to shift her mood.

Joseph Jaworsky, in his book, *Synchronicity*, ties the inter-relational qualities of confidence, purpose, commitment, and surrendering judgment together so well in the following words:

"In my old way of operating, I was very clear about my capacity to commit to something. Commitment meant being highly disciplined in sticking with something. I had been taught early on that the way you win lawsuits is to make it happen, outwork the other person, stick with it, and stay deeply committed to what you are doing. This is the kind of commitment where you seize fate by the throat and do whatever it takes to succeed.

It was only later that I began to understand another, deeper aspect of commitment. This kind of commitment begins not with will, but with willingness. We begin to listen to the inner voice that helps guide us as our journey unfolds. The underlying component of this kind of commitment is our trust in the playing out of our destiny. We have the integrity to stand in a "state of surrender," as Varela put it, knowing that whatever we need at the moment to meet our destiny will be available to us. It is at this point that we alter our relationship with the future.

When we operate in this state of commitment, we see ourselves as an essential part of the unfolding of the universe. In this state of being our life is naturally infused with meaning, and as Buber says, we sacrifice our "puny, unfree will" to our "grand will.

Out of this commitment, a certain flow of meaning begins. People gather around you, and a larger conversation begins to form. When you are in this state of surrender, this state of wonder, you exert an enormous attractiveness—not because you are special, but because people are attracted to authentic presence and to the unfolding of a future that is full of possibilities."

The more one studies the self in a quest to understand who "I" am, the more one begins to realize that there is no "I" at all. The "I" is just part of a larger cosmos of interconnected beings. As one finds their path and begins to walk with grace and clarity, suspending the mental chatter that goes with mediocrity, the more synchronicity follows. A creative energy begins to assist you.

INTENTION

If you follow your bliss, you put yourself on a kind of track
that has been there all the while, waiting for you, and the
life that you ought be living is the one you are living. When
you can see that, you begin to meet people who are in the
field of your bliss and they open the doors to you.

—Joseph Campbell

My youngest daughter, Paloma, was taking a nap in her playpen while I was working Cairo in the midday sun. The sand in the arena reflected the heat and the horses in the near pasture grazed quietly. Cairo was a young, grey Arabian gelding. He was a sensitive and intelligent horse. We were preparing for an upcoming dressage show and were working on our transitions. I was focusing on balancing and smoothing the transition from the trot-to-canter, canter-to-trot, while changing directions. I was feeling frustrated because Cairo was making the transitions before I asked him.

He did this several times and at first I discouraged him from changing his stride or direction before I had made the request. I felt like he was changing the program before I had given him a cue to do so. One of the *traditional* rules of horsemanship is that a horse should *not* do something before it is asked of him. After several attempts to get our transitions coordinated, I started to feel perplexed. Cairo was a good horse—a willing and eager partner. He wasn't trying to be bad.

I started thinking that perhaps *I* was sending some cue to him that I was unaware of that was causing him to change prematurely. So I got curious and stripped away any cues I could think of. I didn't change my hands or legs. I monitored the subtle shifts in my body weight and breath. Still he would change prematurely.

I began to realize that he was changing his stride or his direction when I was thinking about changing. Just like the birds of prey I had worked with for so many years, he was responding to my mental images before I was even aware I was having them. As soon as I created an intention that had an image of him changing stride, he would change. He was listening to my desire to change.

The words of my first dressage teacher drummed through my head "Use your seat!" And then, the words of my Richard when he teaches aikido *"Blend* your center with the center of your training partner." Cairo wanted to become one with me as much as I with him. My training of Cairo, or rather *his* training of *me*, gave new clarity to the *power of intention*.

Intention is comprised of our passion or desire to manifest. Intention has energy—it has *life*. Intention is directly connected to our spiritual self. We may have no cognitive awareness of our intent and yet it is like an energy humming inside of us.

The horse, being an energetic wizard, listens to our inner intentions and desires with a deep sense of awareness. When our desire is strong and clear, the horse follows our intention, as if no other leadership quality were needed. Their sophisticated ability to listen to this *inner longing* has always fascinated me and encouraged me to inquire deeper into this phenomenon. What, then, makes up intention? How is intention distinguished from wishful thinking or wanting?

I have seen over and over again with my clients that *wanting* something doesn't mean anything to a horse—there is nothing that they can connect with. A wish is a figment of the imagination. It is isolated to the confines of the individual's fantasy. It has no relational context to the greater morphogenic field—other beings don't recognize the opportunity to contribute to a 'want.'

An example of a wish is "I want to increase my earnings by twenty thousand dollars this year." The horse responds by saying, "O.K., that sounds nice, I hope it works out for you. I do not see any way I can assist you." On the other hand, an intention has a more encompassing purpose, "I am a commitment to buying a house to take care of my family and (to do so) I will increase my earnings by twenty thousand dollars by the end of this year." Having twenty thousand more dollars doesn't mean anything, whereas the commitment to take care of one's family has a lot of meaning. Other people immediately understand the value of such a commitment.

I like to think of intention as an arrow that you send out into the world. By bringing our deeper drives into the foreground we begin to sharpen our arrow. We refine it as we go, like chiseling the shards of the flint, giving our intention form and shape. The more our intention has shape, the more the invisible energetic forces of the morphogenic field and the *greater mystery* can galvanize around our desire and assist us in bringing it into form. The mystery of synchronicity resides in this playing field.

WHAT IS MY TRUE INTENTION?

Amy was a tall brown-haired woman in her early thirties. She was training to be a professional coach. Her outside story was that she wanted to become a qualified coach and take over her mother-in-law's coaching practice. As she prepared to team up with the horse she spoke to the group about her plan. It sounded like a good story, but her intention lacked life.

I found my attention wandering. I wondered why I felt so disinterested —I checked to see if the horse felt a similar lack of enthusiasm. Indeed, Skip, a bay gelding living at the ranch I was visiting in Colorado, was looking in another direction.

I tried to draw out Amy's inner passion by asking her, "Why do you think Skip is looking in the other direction? He keeps looking away from you when you talk."

She insisted on staying focused on her vision, "I want to become a great coach. I have invested a significant amount of my time, energy and money on this endeavor already."

Her body told a different story. Her eyes looked dull, her face almost sullen. She rested on her left leg, as if only partially standing. She didn't seem ready to enter into a deeper speculation about her more inner desires. Knowing we weren't going anywhere by talking about it, I let her go out into the center of the arena to work Skip.

She declared her commitment to take over her mother-in-law's coaching practice. Skip stood quietly and stared at her. She asked him to move forward. Skip did not respond. In fact, it looked like he was taking a nap. By his very inertia he reflected back to her that her outer intention lacked life. He had moved for everyone else, why wasn't Skip moving for her?

She asked him to move forward again. This time he looked at her as if to ask, "What do you really care about?" She persisted several times to no avail. Skip had confirmed my suspicions that her outer story did not match her inner life force. She was stuck and the only authentic thing to do was enter into the gap between her external agenda and her inner intention. What was missing?

I translated that Skip perhaps could not see her vision and that he kept looking away from her when she spoke. I asked, "Is his looking away from you a reflection of you looking away from your commitment to take on your mother-in-law's coaching practice?"

Amy began to cry. The whole group felt her frustration. They were poised at the edge of their seat as if their own forward thrust might help her find her inner voice.

As she wept, words formed and she exhaled, "I want to have a baby."

Aha! Now we were all interested again, the whole group took a deep sigh of relief.

"Tell us about that," I said.

"I just really want to start a family with my husband," she said. "I'm afraid that this isn't what everyone else wants to hear."

Skip's persistent lack of interest allowed her to take ownership of the fact that her heart wasn't in being a coach. She had resisted making this confession because she had already invested so much of herself and felt it was the culturally acceptable thing to do.

The group supported the notion that starting a family was also a leadership declaration. And Skip, as if acknowledging this realization, nudged Amy as if to say, "Let's go." It took Amy a few minutes to let go of the preconceived expectations she had set for herself. She went out to work Skip with this new declaration and he enthusiastically began to trot for her.

While Amy's inner desire to start a family did not match her outer story of what she *should* do, she did not show up to Skip as inauthentic. He didn't listen to the words she spoke; he listened to her life force, which was *looking in another direction*. He was mirroring an inner state that Amy already embodied.

Upon further conversations Amy shared that the idea of becoming a coach was overwhelming to her. Her first forays at coaching were unfulfilling. Somewhere inside she was already questioning her self-imposed sense of obligation to *stick with it*.

Amy's inner longing already had intention. The horse, Skip, was responding to her energetic cues by placing his body in the new direction she was already internally in. Once she made a decision to move in this new direction, the energy of her intention was readily available, explaining Skip's ease in movement in her latter attempts to engage with him.

INTUITION

It is by logic that we prove,
But by intuition that we discover.

— Henry Poincare

One morning I came down to the barn later than usual. Rather than feed the horses, I decided to walk to the south end of the barn. I felt the cool mist of the morning fog on my face and smelled the rye grass in the field. I wasn't thinking about anything, I was just *being* the environment around me.

I became drawn to the property line and started walking the fence. I usually never walk this line since it is somewhat remote. As I walked down towards the brambles, a big brown body caught my attention. It was Lacey's oldest daughter, Lily, but something was wrong. She should be up with the other horses waiting for her morning flake of hay. She was standing still as if she were a wax statue. My alarm increased as I ran towards her. (Horses don't stand still with their back turned to you when they hear or see you coming. They turn to face you.) As I quickly approached I lowered my voice and called softly to her, sensing that something was very wrong and I did not want her to move.

Sure enough, she was caught in the fence. Her knee was gashed open as if she had tried to struggle before realizing that it was futile. I ran back to the barn, breathing hard, and grabbed the fence cutters and a halter. When I returned she was as statuesque as I had left her. She quietly allowed me to cut the wire and take her leg out of the twisted tangle. I placed the halter on her and slowly walked her back to the barn. Her injuries were serious and she almost died from a bone infection in the months that followed. It took over six months to heal the deep gash in her knee.

Another time I left my habitual path of daily chores and found myself wandering an entirely different fence, only to find my fox terrier caught in a neighbor's coyote trap. A tight wire was wrapped around his neck slowly choking him. If I had not followed some unknown cue to walk to an area I rarely travel, I never would have found him and he would have died a terrible, slow death.

Many more times I have come into the barn and just felt like something was amiss. I would feel my guts, get out of my head and just move to where some unknown energy drew me only to find a watering trough that was bone dry because some part had broken.

Why was I drawn to these outer edges? What drew me to follow the fence or feel like something was wrong in the barn?

The *Encyclopedia Britannica* defines intuition as the power of obtaining knowledge that cannot be acquired either by inference or observation, by reason or experience. Intuition is an independent source of knowledge that we cannot exactly define or quantify, a *precognitive knowing* of oneself in relation to the outer world. It is informed by energetic sensations and responses. It arises out of the unknown landscape of our physical being and the energy of the environment around us. If we allow our intuition to enter into our cognitive space uncensored by our historic conditioning it can inform us in profound ways.

Mowlana Jalaluddin Rumi (1207–1273) wrote the following:

> *"There are two kinds of intelligence: One acquired,*
> *As a child in school memorizes facts and concepts*
> *From books and from what the teacher says,*
> *Collecting information from the traditional sciences*
> *As well as from the new sciences.*
>
> *With such intelligence you rise in the world.*
> *You get ranked to your competence in retaining*
> *Information. You stroll with this intelligence*
> *In and out of fields of knowledge, getting always more*
> *Marks on your preserving tablets.*

There is another kind of tablet, one
Already completed and preserved inside you.
A spring overflowing its springbox. A freshness
In the center of the chest. This other intelligence
Does not turn yellow or stagnate. It's fluid,
And it doesn't move from outside to inside
Through the conduits of plumbing—learned.

This second knowing is a fountainhead
From within you, moving out."

I have asked many of the CEOs and executives I work with how they make the difficult decisions they face as leaders and they all report that they 'just' have a gut feeling about it. And they use the word 'just' as if it were no big deal. They *just* had an intuition. It was that simple. They also report the numerous times they haven't listened to their intuition and the failures they've experienced as a result. Think of the times you've heard yourself or someone say, "I just have a gut-feeling about it," and often you respect that response.

We often recognize intuitive information only in hindsight. We realize we had a sense about something, but we did not follow it. Or we respond to our intuition and nothing bad actually happens, there is no affirmation. How can we learn to allow our intuition to be a stronger informant?

By developing the capacity to listen to our intuition, we can *relax* into self-leadership. We allow our internal intelligence to inform and assist us. In this authentic state of mind, we create a *spaciousness* in which we sense when things are on track and when unspoken breakdowns exist within ourselves or the herd (team). We can intuit the subtle shifts in the tone of the marketplace. *We can lead by following, and follow the lead.*

When we are in an intuitive state of mind, our senses are not clogged with the judge's mental chatter. We are not thinking. We are just *being present* to our inner calling. When we listen to our intuition there is effortlessness or grand simplicity. When we don't, we spend days, weeks, or even years punishing ourselves for not paying attention to that *below the radar* feeling that we didn't follow. How can we forgive ourselves and regain our basic animal right to sense the world from an energetic perspective?

Given that wild animals rely on their intuitive responses as their primary source of information, we might ask what happened to us? Why don't we respect this precognitive information? Why don't we listen to it, honor and respect it? Why have we become numb to our sensate wisdom? It is as if we have become intuitively impaired compared to the rest of our animal brothers. We are each born with instinct, intuition and sensate wisdom. But it literally gets taught out of us from birth on.

Many highly intuitive people are raised to think that their sensitivity is wrong or problematic. Some try to turn off their raw anima responses by internalizing it and developing a rich inner, fantasy world full of fairies and spirit creatures. Others try to voice their feelings louder, usually creating more discipline and ridicule. If family or friends overly criticize them for their sensate expression, they tend to develop a social awkwardness that further distances them from feeling *normal*. Many only feel safe with animals. Humans become scary, lying animals that cannot be relied upon or trusted.

Animals know that their lives depend on listening to their intuition—their sixth, seventh, eight and ninth senses—to gauge safety versus danger; foe or friend. They would not, could not, turn off their sensate responses even if punished for its expression. Why? Because it is their primary informant, the way they create their reality whereas, the human animal uses words in addition to sensate or somatic expression. This is where trouble can start, especially when the words used by the person speaking do not match their somatic expression; in other words their body language is not matching their words. This is a recipe for disaster for highly intuitive humans, for their sensate responses are picking up the discrepancy. The lie between the words and the body creates an *elephant in the room*.

Animals, particularly horses, are competent teachers for us in developing our intuition, since they live and breath through their intuition. They expect us to communicate with our *feeling body* because this is the way they communicate.

Horses want to know what we believe—right now—this moment. Horses have no tolerance for us when we are in our head trying to remember what we believe. When we are in our head, they sense that we are not in our *feeling body*.

As animals we are born with the *right* to respect our intuition. At one time we, too, depended on our intuition and energetic responses to stimuli for our survival—this trait still reside inside us—often rusty and uncared for.

Children come into the world with a wonderful innocence and connection to the universal field of energy. Our pride for their raw sense of knowing speaks into our own longing to have that same innocence again. Unfortunately, our cultures and social systems often deny these important qualities. In fact, as a species we teach our children and ourselves not to respect our intuition.

A common example is the five-year-old who says to her distressed mother, "What's the matter, mommy?" And the mother replies sternly, "Nothing is the matter!" The child thinks to herself that what she is feeling must be incorrect. The mother's quick response to her concern disrespects her intuitive feelings that her mother is upset.

As parents, with all the good intentions in the world, we often do not realize that we have dishonored the intuitive feelings of our children. The mother may have thought she was protecting her child from uncomfortable feelings. But these untruthful responses to the inquiries of those around us reinforce the sense that our intuition is unreliable.

We grow up believing that what our parents, friends and elders say is *true* until we no longer respect our own intuitive process. It is still there but we don't listen to it, we don't trust it anymore. We may not even notice that our body is in a fight-or-flight response. We lose the skill of speaking from our *feeling body* because we often cannot ground our perceptions in factual experience, or we don't trust that others will believe us.

When we have an intuition, we often negate it quickly with a story that we must have missed something, or better yet, we are just being paranoid. We repeat what we have learned, often telling people the easy answer to their questions and avoiding the real conversation.

Because of the overwhelming social pressure to negate our feelings, we often don't realize that we have made judgments about others and ourselves based on our sensate perceptions. We tend to rationalize our decisions with socially accepted stories that become convoluted and isolating.

As a culture, we don't hold another's intuitive concerns as a virtue and thus do not respond with a care for their intuition. How many times can you recall when a friend or loved one asked you if you were upset and you shrugged them off with a trite answer? Does this take care of their dignity? Does it take care of yours?

Studying and relating to animals can retrain and refine our intuition. To open the cog ways for this kind of exploration and discovery, we can learn to listen like an animal, and more important, to trust what we feel.

A PERSONAL STORY

My own failures have been a result of not listening to my intuition. The one time I can boast of being kicked by a horse in all of my years of working with them came out of a cocky disregard for my sixth sense.

It was the night before an important horseshow. I had bathed Lacy and blanketed her before putting her back in the pasture to eat dinner. Even though it was dinnertime and normally she would rush to her food—she ran around the field with her ears pinned back throwing her body onto the ground with a thug; rolling over and over, trying to rub the blanket off her back. As she got up her blanket was a disheveled rag laying in a disastrous mess atop her back. I knew it was an accident waiting to happen—I had to fix it. She was clearly pissed about the blanket. I knew better than to approach her. My sixth sense was screaming, "This is not the time to approach this horse!" My cognitive mind was trying to assist by replying, "Get a halter and get the horse in a safe manner."

My next action to approach this angry horse came out of a cocky attitude that overrode my physical intuitive guide—I decided to do it anyway, just to see. She was in the field eating as I approached her with the intent of fixing her blanket. I did not anticipate that she would actually take an additional step back to put me in my place. She kicked my right leg mid-femur, landing me on the ground. I lay in a humbled heap on the ground not quite able to move my leg—all those months of training wasted on a foolish moment of overriding my natural sensibility.

My cocky disregard for her mood landed me with a dent in my leg that I will have for the rest of my life. It is a reminder to stay awake to my intuition, perhaps the most important informant I have. Now when I recognize my cocky attitude, I am alert that maybe it is trying to override a more natural intuition that is resting just below the surface.

When we train our intuition and listen to its wisdom we have to be careful of our mind's desire to take over with its know-it-all stance, because arrogance and cockiness are not the only persuasive interferers. Yet another trickster that tampers with intuition is our mental game of paranoia. As we bring our intuition back into the foreground as a sensate resource we have to learn to distinguish intuition from paranoia. Paranoia arises out of a sensation of fear. Our body feels fear and our mind quickly creates stories about *why* we are feeling this way. Unfortunately, paranoia often displaces this fear onto *something (or someone) out there*.

The simplest way to distinguish intuition from paranoia or arrogance is to see if there is a story associated with the intuitive information. Intuition does not have a story. It arises out of the great nowhere, the universal field. We can't quite explain *why* we feel uneasy. Paranoia is often associated with recurrent stories we have about the world or others. When working with horses, you don't have time to be paranoid. Your only effective tool is your intuition and your response to that information.

INTUITIVE OR PSYCHIC

Some equine practitioners have witnessed the amazing intuitive powers of horses enough to truly know that horses offer a profound look at the inside of the human being—that their timing and response is beyond coincidence—beyond scientific reason. Others still grapple with trying to *understand* and figure out what is really going on. Is it even possible to truly understand how horses know so much about us or why they are so unconditionally accepting of our clumsiness? Does it really matter that we figure it out? Certainly the answer does not lie in our *logical mind*.

In the summer of 2003, flying to Minnesota to teach a clinic, I read the question "Are horses psychic?" posed in a recently published article. Having watched thousands people work with horses and have the horses offer different responses that seemed directly correlated to each person's current life situation, I can reasonably answer "yes" to that question. But explaining the phenomenon of psychic reflection to someone who has never seen it is another story.

Once the public clinic was over, I worked privately with four students who were learning how to incorporate Equine Guided Education into their coaching practice, and subsequently had the opportunity to witness the psychic lives of horses in a new light. We were in an enclosed arena and had selected Grace, a brown mare, to work with us. It just so happened that an old, grey Arabian gelding was also in the ring, but since his pasture was far away and our time was precious, I decided to let him stay loose in the arena with us, figuring that he would take a nap in the corner.

THE OLD GREY GELDING

Judy was the first to be the practice client. She took Grace in hand and stood in front of us and spoke about how she needed to move forward with divorcing her husband. She had settled on this decision over a year ago, but had continued to reside in the same household with him. She declared that she needed to move her husband into action around getting the divorce.

I questioned, "Why do you feel you need to move him? Why not focus on what you need to do rather than waiting for him to do something?"

She agreed and re-declared that she would take the next action towards separation. Just as she was about to move into the lunging circle, the old grey came out of his stupor and quietly blocked her path. She tried to move him out of her way, but he just circled around her. They circled together five or six times until she let out a huge sigh and just walked around him in a mood of frustration.

She walked away from him and created a new circle to lunge Grace in. The old grey stood just outside her circle and fell asleep. Amused by the coincidence, we projected that the old grey was her husband standing quietly near her circle while she went on with her life.

Next came Tim. He brought Grace over to us and was just about to speak his declaration when the old grey came out of the corner of the arena and quite purposefully placed his body between Tim and us so that we could not see Tim. I have seen horses do this when humans are trying to hide themselves from others. Knowing Tim from several other occasions I thought this was pertinent to how Tim approached new groups of people. He would first hide out until he felt safe speaking personally about himself. I thought to myself, "How funny, the grey came out at just the right time to mirror Tim's desire to be hidden."

Greg was the third person to go and had never worked with horses in this way before. He was a special guest of Tim's and had been invited to this private session in appreciation for his help putting together the public clinic. The old grey had gone back to his corner of the arena and was napping. Greg spoke about how he was running his family's business and that he really did not want to do that anymore. He wanted to start his own business, but he was afraid to let his father down.

I asked him what his new business ideas were. Even though I knew he knew, he was not forthcoming. He began a long-winded story about what was not working in his life and how he felt responsible for taking care of the family business. I was having a hard time finding his center, both physically and emotionally. I asked Greg, "Let us assume that you have decided not to work in the family business anymore. What are you centering your future business on?"

Before I had finished my words, the old grey gelding came out of his slumber and sauntered into the center of the lunging circle. He took over the center of the circle that was supposed to be Greg's defining place. The 'center' of the lunging circle is very important, as it is the first step in lunging a horse to establish the center of the circle, which becomes a metaphor of centering on your goals. When the horse enters the center it is usually a reflection that the human is either asking someone else to lead or someone else is running the show.

Eric realized that the old grey taking his center reflected the same issue that he was having with his father. Greg was not taking a stand for his place in the business—or anything else, for that matter. His father was asking Greg to be responsible for the business, but was not giving him the room to do it in his own way. The old grey gelding's reflection allowed Greg to put into words the leadership move that he needed to make with his father and he proceeded to politely but firmly move the old gelding out of the center of the lunge circle so that he could run the business with Grace.

The last to go was Ed, a successful software developer for small businesses. He had developed several organizational models that had proven to be quite successful. He was in the time of his life when he wanted to teach others what he knew and create a team that would continue his work collectively. He sent Grace around the lunge circle at a steady trot. Grace and Ed moved in unity together. Their movements were graceful and they were clearly satisfied with the team they had created together. Out of nowhere came the old grey, trotting along *between* Ed and Grace as if he wanted to be part of the team.

Fascinating! Now, it is safe to say that we are projecting our own interpretations onto the grey's interaction with each person. But how do we explain how the old grey, who had never met these four people—who can't speak English—, responded entirely differently with each person and reflected what each person needed to see? He could have just as easily taken a nap in the corner, as we had expected him to do.

It is unexplainable from a western science perspective. But it was amazing to witness. And the grey helped each person gain insights and see new moves they could make in their lives.

CURIOSITY

Anything forced and misunderstood can never be beautiful.
—Xenophon, 444 B.C.

Filly #17 was bought at an auction. No one knew her name or history. The only thing known was her pedigree, which revealed that she came from a long line of very athletic superstars in the western cow horse sports. One knew more about her grandparents than they did about her. She displayed the same talent of movement that her line was known for.

Unfortunately, she was on the fast track to being a horse that nobody wanted. She was too valuable to give up on yet. Besides she was only two years old. She was sent to me because everyone else had given up on her. I was her last hope. I had a reputation for fixing problem horses and repairing a horse's willingness to partner.

Unlike my human clients, Filly #17 could not tell me her story through words. The only thing I could rely on was my ability to listen for her history, her story about the human, and her own sense of self. I had to listen, not to what I saw on paper or heard in conversation, but to what my sixth sense said about her. I knew it was important not to let my own ideals influence the listening required to find her true nature.

I noticed her kind eye first. She was affectionate; the desire to partner was still there, but I could tell that she had gotten lost. Her coat was soft as silk; obviously she had been well fed. Her beauty in movement inspired me. Her ears at full attention told me that she was curious and wanted to make contact. But at any attempt to lead her into partnership where she had to connect with me, her ears went back and she dug her hooves into the ground.

The weeks that followed were no easy feat. I applied various techniques of colt starting. I was gentle and encouraging, asking only for simple maneuvers. She would often respond by rearing up with her front legs pawing the air in an effort to intimidate me. I tried to give her something to do that would occupy her attention and keep her mind on the task at hand rather than on me. When I asked her to move forward on a long line she would turn her back to me so that all I could see was her butt. She resisted any attempts at activities that required her to pay attention and partner up with me.

The more I insisted she listen to me, the more she just as furiously insisted I listen to her. I could see that she didn't know how to partner and resented any attempts on my part to encourage her to do so. She was basically saying, "*I don't want to play.*" The task of changing her mind was going to be harder than I thought.

She lacked social skills—I began to realize that she had most likely never been given the opportunity to bond with other horses and learn her place in the herd. Perhaps she had even been taken away from her mother too early because it was apparent that she didn't know how to relate to others, horse or human. It was as if she thought she was the only intelligent being in the space and I was merely an object to avoid.

I decided to simplify things and focused on the simple principles of giving her clear requests, clear guidelines and clear consequences for not teaming up with me. This failed. Her bad attitude dominated every interaction. The traditional methods of colt starting were not working. Even my first forays in experimentation were ineffective. It was pointless to get angry with her and force her into a mold. My horse wisdom reminded me that she was a unique being with her own mind and her own approach to harmony. All I had to do was find it. I was determined not to lose this filly and her brilliant potential.

I knew from my years of working with horses that when I get frustrated with the horse it usually means that I have lost the game;

I am being ineffective in my leadership. My goal is to create an environment for the horse where the horse feels like she is accomplishing something so that I can build on positive reinforcement. If the horse is failing, then I am failing as the leader of the team. She was losing, and the everyday approach to starting a young horse wasn't working. So, I threw out my textbook notions about horse training, and got curious.

Knowing I didn't know the answer forced me to become playful and experiment. The moment she became resistant, I knew I was missing something, and that was the moment I could create a new outcome. My imagination was my only card left. I had great faith that by being present, open and connected to her I could find a way to lead her to partnership. I still wasn't sure what type of partnership we would end up with, but my dream was strong. Failure was not an option, and I knew my only hope for success lay in *not knowing* and not getting caught in the way things should be going.

Now I had to really laugh at myself. If I ever wanted a challenge, here she was. She was my gift, a reflection of myself. The Great Spirit had handed me my next lesson in looking beyond the obvious. I knew the solution lay not in fighting with her, but respecting her quirks and her fierce need for her own authority. It was my job to create this possibility through my willingness to listen to what worked for her.

She, like people who have had big betrayals of trust in their early years, look into the world ready for the fight. The fight for self-respect and self-boundary becomes a *vigilance* against other people's attempts to define her world.

Filly #17 had no respect for her human counterpart and was more focused on holding her own position than to listening to my offer of a new kind of relationship. This is the most difficult type of situation to turn around in horses and people. They have already decided that people are unreliable, dishonest and perhaps even dangerous. Their strategy of choice is to rebel against any attempts to stereotype or train them.

She revealed to me that somewhere along the line her previous human had failed to lead her, had indeed confused her, and she had grown resentful of any attempt by another human to take the lead. Just like a person who is conditioned by their experiences, she held a troubled history in the sinews of her flesh that presented as a mood of resentment.

As I asked her try new things, she first said, *"No, I won't— and you can't make me."*

I gently encouraged her, *"I have all the confidence in the world that you can."*

I had to embody confidence and consistency, so that she could learn to rely on my commitment to bring out her beauty. To do this, I had to trust myself and have complete faith that she would listen back in kind. I wasn't afraid of things being messy, or trying something new. I had to imagine that success may not look like my first picture of it, but if I remained flexible she and I could find it together.

My challenge was to rekindle her desire to be part of a team, to rebuild trust that had been broken and to encourage a positive mood toward the human. As long as she lived in a mood of resentment, any attempts to partner with her would be futile. Her lack of a clear story of her purpose in life had created a self-imposed wall of isolation. She had not yet accepted the human as a worthy partner. In fact, she was avoiding the conversation of partnering altogether.

If I respected her history, as I did with my clients, I didn't need to react to it. I asked myself, "Is this her mind, body or spirit talking to me?" By looking at her patterns of behavior, performance and perception of possibility, I could work through her narrow habits. I knew she wanted to be somebody, to do something valuable. I could feel in her heart she wanted to change, to end her isolation.

As the weeks unfolded I slowly gained her trust. When I found myself getting frustrated I would change the game. I avoided getting set in my agenda about what a horse trainer *should do*. I let my intuitive mind take over and inform me of the next playing field. I stayed focused on the first and most important goal at hand—that she become curious about me and who I was to her.

I noticed that she liked to follow energy. I set up scenarios where I would ask her to listen to me; where was I going, what energy was I being? I kept grabbing her attention. As she responded with curiosity she would get rewarded and moments of bonding would happen. Our experiences of positive socializing began to build on each other and we were becoming friends. As long as I remained curious and open, she responded in turn.

I paid careful attention not to push her too fast or too far. I respected her, and at the same time, I held a firm ground of acceptable and unacceptable performance, just like a lead mare would do. I did silly, unconventional things with her, and I continued to bypass her expectation that I was going to force her into something.

One day I slipped onto her bareback. No saddle, no bridle. It just felt like the right thing to do. She didn't even notice. The minute my mind would attempt to analyze the situation or that cocky chick on my right shoulder began to think she was doing a good job, I could feel the filly's muscles tighten and bunch, ready to spring. Each time I let go of my *knowing mind* and stayed with my animal body, agenda-less, she would soften and her ears would go forward.

She started to impress me with her intelligence. Sometimes I would laugh aloud, wondering who was teaching whom. As long as I stayed away from any preconceived notions of who she was and how I *should* lead her, she was more present than I could have hoped for. I'd found the keys to her freedom, and she'd found mine. My work with this filly confirmed my belief that leadership is not confined to formulas, tools or theories. To assume that we can lead by intellect alone is the first step in losing the most essential leadership quality that we each have inside us, our innate birthright—our intuitive body. And yet it is the hardest to trust and develop because there is no rulebook.

Maybe that is why the novice equestrian or the amateur leader often prefers the tips and techniques found in books. In their naivety they hope that the 1-2-3's and ABC's of horsemanship will give them the information they need to succeed. I'm not saying that these metrics are not important or useful. On the contrary, they give our Cartesian mind something to grasp onto. But to become proficient and masterful, we can only rely on *who we are* behind the rope, and in the saddle.

A person's willingness to accept this responsibility reveals the difference between an amateur and a person training towards mastery. This filly provides testimony to this, for all of the ABC's failed; the only answer was *in not having one*.

Filly #17, now fondly called Tess, represents the other person who responds to our gestures of interaction: who feels the outcome of our gestures: the "other" holding the rope. It's not the rope she responds to, or the pressure I apply with the rope. It is the mood of possibility and flexibility I *extend* through the rope. It's my willingness to let my idea become her idea. And sometimes to allow her idea to become my idea.

It's a hard and often lonely road. It's far easier to rely on steps 1-2-3 and then fault the system or the horse when it is not working. It is much harder to be honest with yourself and see that *you* may be the limitation.

MIND, BODY AND SPIRIT

A good friend once told me that she felt that working with
horses is like being on a long trip.
It's a journey with no destination—an unending process—
and everything that is important is 'as you go,'
Not when 'you get there.'
—*Mark Rashid*

Tess reminded me of a young man I worked with many years ago. Sam was a bright, handsome man in his mid-thirties. He came from a prestigious family in Canada. He was newly married and flitting from job to job.

He bore an air of entitlement as if people should take him seriously, based simply on his family background. He postured that people should accept him as a leader because *he thought* he had something to offer. He wanted to be granted the authority to lead because he was born from a line of leaders and yet had never proven his ability to do so (similar to filly #17).

Subsequently, he resented employer after employer because they could not see that he was important. He wasn't open to seeing his own reflection, that his mood of resentment pushed away his boss and made him difficult to work with.

WHAT'S IN AN ATTITUDE?

During his attendance in management training at the ranch, Sam set out to work with Sadie. Sadie has been a teacher of humans for years. Her generosity of spirit and amazing patience has always inspired me.

He made a declaration that leading Sadie represented his goal of receiving a promotion at work. He had learned by doing this exercise the previous summer that the horse only listened to who he was being inside, not what he felt he deserved.

To my wonder this usually kind, gentle mare dropped her head, dulled her eyes and dragged her feet around the circle. I noticed that she was going along begrudgingly in a sour mood, as if saying, "If only he was a better boss, I could be a better horse."

"So Sam," I offered, "I think she is portraying you. You are now your boss trying to lead someone like you."

"I think you're onto something," he replied.

"What does it feel like to have this horse dragging her feet and giving only the smallest part of herself?"

He could see that she was not thrilled to be led by him. He could not deny the thousand pounds of mood before his eyes. Even though she was going through the moves, would he want to keep her on his team? Did he want to promote her and give her more responsibility?

He got the message loud and clear, since he knew that the horse had no agenda with him. She was only reflecting him. I silently thanked Sadie for showing him something that other humans couldn't seem to get across.

After years of blaming his numerous bosses, he began to see his own responsibility in how his career was turning out. He wasn't getting promoted because of his presentation, not because his bosses were thoughtless.

Sam saw through Sadie's mirroring that he presented to his employers a begrudging attitude—a predisposed notion that it was their responsibility to please him. He had forgotten that to be part of an effective team, he had to come to the table with a willing attitude and something to offer.

The first step for Sam in developing a leadership presence was to identify his somatic patterns of thought, behavior and possibility along the dimensions of mind, body and spirit as shown in diagram 1. The next phase was for Sam to identify which patterns were inhibiting his ability to progress. Once his limiting issues were identified, Sam made a set of commitments to develop new practices along the somatic dimensions as listed in diagram 2.

Sadie's honest reflections provided grounded feedback for him as he learned to integrate his desire to be of value with the needs of his employers.

This new way of bringing forward his spirit of engagement paved the way to becoming a team player that other people wanted to work with. In subsequent private sessions we continued to work on shifting his perspective from "how he thought his employers were doing," to "how *he* was doing."

He practiced bringing a mood of curiosity and willingness to his work. He focused on making offers that added to the team's purpose. He made it a regular practice to ask his boss for feedback, being more interested in her assessments than in his own. This was a significant paradigm shift for this young man and eventually led to him receiving the promotion that he finally earned.

Diagram 1: Identifying somatic patterns

SOMATIC DOMAIN	PATTERNS OF
Mind	Self assessments and judgments Judgments of others
Body	Behavior Performance Mood and attitude
Spirit	Perception of reality Perception of possibility Inner longing to contribute

Diagram 2: Before and after somatic intervention:

SOMATIC DOMAIN	BEFORE SOMATIC INTERVENTION	AFTER SOMATIC INTERVENTION
Mind	Interpretation #1: I am entitled to be a leader Interpretation #2: It is my boss's fault that I am not getting promoted	Interpretation #1: I earn my place as a leader through my actions Interpretation #2: It is my responsibility to earn my boss's respect
Body	Mood: resentful, begrudging Shoulders stiff, eyes rigid	Mood: curious, willing Eyes soft, shoulders relaxed
Spirit	I desire to be a leader	I desire to develop myself as producing value to others through taking responsibility for my actions and their results

Leadership of the self resides in our flesh as mood and energetic tone. The lack of flow or harmony is not so much a reflection of what is happening on the outside, but of what is believed on the inside. Being able to act with choice—rather than reacting—requires a commitment to practicing leadership as a physical phenomenon rather than an intellectual exercise.

Developing this somatic awareness means attending to our mind, body and spirit as a whole system. Our mind attempts to understand itself and make sense of our environment: our body responds to the environment: our spirit fosters our underlying inspiration for possibility and meaning. Connecting to the natural world—we are reminded that our inner spirit has its own voice—and we are persistently propelled forward by an unconscious desire to make a contribution.

It is not enough to change the way we think. In Sam's example, it was not enough for him to decide to be *less resentful*. Our spirit is our underlying inspiration for possibility and meaning. He had to find a way to acknowledge his spiritual longing to be valued as a leader and do the work through demonstrating the leadership qualities of confidence, intention, curiosity in others and earning respect through consistent and reliable action.

In all my years of studying leadership and horsemanship, whether I am in the world of my animal friends or that of people, I keep coming back to the same place the poets speak of—the answers to the meaning of life reside in the natural world.

Ultimately, we are at the whim of Mother Nature. When we let go of what we know for *what we don't know*, our imagination keeps us afloat through the various tidal changes of our lives.

CONCLUSION

Until one has loved an animal,
A part of one's soul remains unawakened.
-Anatole France

We are not so different from our animal brothers. In fact, we need them more than we know. They remind us of being alive, truly alive. They remind us that life is precious. To have lived a good life is to have wholeheartedly contributed the best parts of ourselves to the greater good.

What is important to us throughout our lifetime changes. Change is as constant as the sun rising and setting each day. Becoming aware of how we apply ourselves to our changing circumstances gives us choice and power. Leveraging our animal nature and developing our nonverbal communicators brings force and momentum to our awareness.

I hope this book brings insight to the qualities of presence that allow our whole body to be alive as we propel ourselves forward. I hope we can learn to *feel* more and stay curious, instead of being so thoughtful all the time. While our language has created many boons for our specie's success, it also has a shadow side. It brings with it the capacity to separate us from the rest of the world.

As we enter this new century we are entering a shift in consciousness. Several generations from now we will begin to see what the seeds of our labor have created. Since 9/11 there has been a dramatic exodus from the workplace world of making more money and working extra hours. People are asking themselves, "*What* do I really care about?" "*Who* do I really care about?" and "*How* do I contribute to the greater good?" I think Mother Theresa's words "*you cannot do great things, you can only do small things with great love"* are becoming enculturated little by little.

People are leaving high-paying jobs and their professional identities to volunteer for the less fortunate, to sing, to dance, to make art, to love animals and nature. These people no longer find integrity with buying the cultural package they were raised with: That more is better; that it is a sign of success to consume *alot*; that it is one man for himself. They are willing to go into what is for them unknown territory, to make do with less, in order to do what they love and to contribute their heart to the greater whole.

What cultural paradigm shift will this create in days to come? When will a schoolteacher make as much money as a lawyer? When will we forgive each other and quit wasting money and resources suing each other? When will men and women of service be respected, appreciated and valued for protecting and caring for the collective? When will they make as much money as doctors and pharmaceutical executives? When will people take a stand for what has heart and meaning and insist that it is as valuable (or perhaps even more valuable) as technology?

When will we be content with saving our own planet instead of looking towards adapting another planet to waste and pillage? When will we collectively learn to simplify our lives, and minimize our consumption? When will we realize that just because we can make it; invent it; or create it; this doesn't mean that it is sustainable—that it has long-term value?

One of my favorite thought leaders and astrologer, Jessica Murray, says it well in her discussion:

> *"It is not as if any one of us, alone, is responsible for coming up with the future. But collectively we are, and collectives are made up of individuals. And each of us, as an individual, is responsible for our own level of awareness.*
>
> *If we believe that reality is created afresh at every moment, it follows that the contents of our minds and hearts must be managed responsibly. Even as we acknowledge as potential realities all the dystopian visions that are swirling around, we must observe them from a distance. Otherwise our fear makes us pump energy into places we*

don't want it to go. By contrast, fear gets crowded out of the picture when we approach the future creatively, with a sense of excitement and a trust in Natural Law.

Climate change is a collective psychic trauma; in the language of psychology, it is a global cry for help. But unlike in the psychotherapeutic model, in this case no external agency can come in and fix us. There are no therapists or family members to stage an intervention. The patient itself, the human race, must do its own healing.

For those who believe that everything in life is a symbol, even catastrophic events can be seen as invitations into an unprecedented state of possibility. To view global warming and its attendant Earth changes this way is to see that an infinite number of potential scenarios are at our disposal. The years ahead start to look not like an ending, but a beginning: a tabula rasa.

Those who have worked therapeutically with visualization and other meditative techniques on an individual level can attest to the fact that they can elicit results that can only be described as magical. We are suggesting that affirmation works in the same way on the collective level. Many spiritual groups will convene during the years ahead to create such visions together (Aquarius); and many single individuals around the world will explore similar imagery alone, the better to pool it psychically. We are not talking about pie-in-the-sky prayers for protection, of the type that dismiss the peril the Earth is in, trying to wish it away like a frightened child. We are talking about aligning our imagery with the forces these transits represent: accepting and honoring them from a place of spiritual maturity.

When the essentially spiritual impulse behind such yearnings is understood, a torrent of creativity is released. What starts as a nagging psychological restlessness becomes the inspiration to pour ourselves into something larger than ourselves: something bigger and more meaningful than our little lives. Immense freedom comes of making contact with the timeless soul that lies behind our time-bound lifetimes. The mundane world then becomes not a prison, but a playground."

What she sees in the stars is what I have heard through the horses' silent message. If we can create reality through our intentions and believe in the energy of commitment and confidence, then we can change our trajectory. It may feel like pulling out an infected tooth without anesthesia, but it is a worthwhile journey. All that is required is that we wake ourselves up; we feel the pain but do not give into it. We trust our vision of a new world in which we are sustainable once again and can live in balance with our other relations. We surrender our ego and the fantasy that we can control our destiny.

We know in our hearts how to do this. But we must stop listening to the old paradigms of what success and accomplishment look like. We must find the courage to take a stand for the simple things—family, gardening, watching the sunrise, taking walks, reading, writing, drawing, sitting in a circle telling stories.

In my work with humans and horses, I see an increasing need for people to re-examine their values at a substantial level. Our values are being challenged to the core. For some, the challenge may come in the form of health, relationships, finances, career identity. I believe that we are all being challenged to let go of the riverbank and allow ourselves to be swept into the stream that is our destiny to follow. Let go of the old judge at the shore telling us we cannot swim, trying to scare us to play it safe.

In the stream we will find other people who believe in what we believe in and we will recognize our collective will. We will gain courage along the way, inviting others into the stream as we gather momentum along the way. We will allow the stream to guide us through the twists and turns of the new landscape of the future. We will find hope in a time of fear. We are our future—mind, body and spirit.

BIBLIOGRAPHY

Abrams, David, *Spell of the Sensuous*. NY: Pantheon Books, 1996.

Adizes, Ichak. *Corporate Life Cycles*. New Jersey: Prentice Hall,1988.

Arien, Angeles, P.h.D. *The Fourfold Way, Walking the Paths of the Warrior, Teacher, Healer, and Visionary*. San Francisco: Harper, 1993.

Armstrong, Thomas. *Seven Kinds Of Smart*. New York: Plume/Penguin, 1993.

Bennett-Goleman, Tara. *Emotional Alchemy*. New York: Harmony Books, 2001.

Budiansky, Stephen. *The Nature of Horses*. New York: The Free Press, 1997.

Curtis, Helena. *Biology*. New York: Worth Publishers, 1979.

Deloria Jr., Vine, and Wildcat, Daniel R. *Power and Place: Indian Education in America*. Colorado: Fulcrum Resources, 2001.

Diamond, Jared. *Guns, Germs and Steel*. New York: W.W. Norton & Co., 1999.

Gatto, John Taylor. *A Different Kind Of Teacher*.

Geer, Andrew. *Reckless*. Self published.

Grandin, Temple and Johnson, Catherine. *Animals in Translation*. NY, Scribner, 2005.

Hearne, Vicki. *Adam's Task*. New York: Vintage, Random House, 1987.

Hillenbrand, Laura. *Seabiscuit*. New York, Random House, 2001.

Hillman, James. *Dream Animals*. San Francisco, Chronicle Books, 1997.

Horowitz, Mardi J. *Cognitive Psychodynamics*. Canada: John Wiley & Sons, 1998.

Horowitz, MD, Mardi J. *Formulation, as a Basis for Planning Psychotherapy Treatment*. Wash. DC, American Psychiatric Press, Inc., 1997.

Jacobsen, Mary-Elaine, Liberating the Everyday Genius. Ballantine, 1999.

Jaworski, Joseph. *Synchronicity*. San Francisco, Berrett-Koehler. 1998.

Kohanov, Linda. *The Tao of Equus*. Novato: New World Library, 2001.

Leider, Richard J. and Shapiro, David A. *Repacking Your Bags*. San Francisco, Berrett Koehler, 2002.

Leonard, George. *Mastery*. New York: Plume, Penguin Books, 1992.

Levine, Dr. Mel, *The Mind Matters*

Maturana & Varela. *Tree of Knowledge*. Boston: Shambala, 1992.

Mc Guane, Thomas. *Some Horses*. NY: Vintage Books, Random House, 2000.

Oliver, Mary. *New and Selected Poems*. Boston: Beacon Press, 1992.

Orr, Ph.D., Robert T. *Vertebrate Biology*. Fifth Edition. Philadelphia: Saunders College Publishing, 1982.

Quammen, David. *The Song of the Dodo*. New York: Touchtone, 1996.

Rashid, Mark. *Horses Never Lie*. Colorado: Johnson Books, 2000.

Sheldrake, Rupert. *Dogs That Know When Their Owners Are Coming Home*. New York: Three Rivers Press, 1999.

Strozzi-Heckler Ph.D., Richard. *The Anatomy of Change, A Way to Move Through Life's Transitions*, Berkeley: North Atlantic Books, 1993.

Strozzi-Heckler, Richard, Ph.D. *Being Human at Work*. Berkeley, North Atlantic Books, 2003

Strozzi-Heckler, Richard Ph.D. *Holding The Center*. Berkeley: North Atlantic Books, 1997.

Swift, Sally. *Centered Riding*. Vermont: A Trafalgar Square Farm Book, 1985.

Vaughan, Terry A. *Mammology*. Second Edition. Philadelphia: Saunders College Publishing, 1978.

Whyte, David. *The House of Belonging*. Washington, Many Rivers Press, 1999.

Whyte, David. *Crossing the Unknown Sea*. New York, Riverhead Books, 2001.

ABOUT THE AUTHOR

Ariana Strozzi is an internationally respected pioneer in the field of Equine Guided Education, and has been bringing the magic of horse communication to people from all walks of life since the 1980's. With innovative vision, Ariana blends equine psychology, biology, somatics, animal behavior and leadership savvy into an experiential format that trains emotional intelligence, self-responsibility, non-verbal communication, authenticity, and intuition.

A Northern California coastal native, Ariana began her horsemanship career at the age of seven, competing in statewide shows. Her talent and versatility quickly recognized, she went on to win championship awards in the English and Western disciplines of eventing, dressage, jumping, reining and working cowhorse.

Ariana supported herself through college training horses and graduated in the major of Zoology with honors from U.C. Davis in 1984 with a specialization in animal behavior and wildlife ecology. She spent several years rehabilitating wild animals and domestic pets. In the early 1980s she innovated the use of physical therapy into the rehabilitation of wild birds of prey at the U.C. Davis Raptor Center, dramatically increasing their releasability back into the wild. After presenting her ideas at several national conferences, physical therapy is now utilized in raptor centers throughout the United States.

In the mid-1980s Ariana became intrigued by the study of leadership and Somatics. She quickly discovered that the concepts of leadership she was learning were grounded in the same principles she used in training horses. In 1989, she brought talent and insight together, founded Leadership & Horses™ and began bringing small business owners and professional leaders out to work with horses and discovered that horses had tremendous ability in reflecting each person's leadership style in a unique and profound way. She went on to coin the term Equine Guided Education in 1999.

Ariana co-founded Strozzi Institute, The Center for Leadership & Mastery, with Richard Strozzi Heckler in the early 1990s and became a Master Somatic Coach in 1996. She co-founded the Equine Guided Education Association™ in 2003. She is an adjunct faculty member for the Institute for Women's' Leadership and resides on several local Board of Directors.

She is the author of *Planning Your Business in the Horse as Healer/Teacher Professions* and the DVD, *Intuitive Horsemanship™* and has been published in *Horse Crazy* and *Being Human at Work*. She currently offers an EGE certification program for incoming professionals in Equine Guided Education and Leadership & Horses™ Program to leaders and teams.

Ariana is an accomplished artist and her illustrations appear in books, on book covers, in magazines and other publications. She lives on a working horse and sheep ranch in the coastal hills of Sonoma County, California with her family.

SKYHORSE RANCH

Nestled in the rolling hills of coastal Sonoma County, SkyHorse Ranch features 200 acres of wildlife and natural surroundings. Visitors include program participants and people who wish to reconnect to the land and enjoy recreational activities including bird watching, kayaking, fishing, bicycling, ranch activities, beach excursions, wine tasting, and artistic expressions.

P. O. Box 415, Valley Ford, CA 94972
Ph/fax 707-876-1908
http://www.SkyHorseRanch.com
http://www.leadershipandhorses.com

EQUINE GUIDED EDUCATION

Ariana Strozzi coined the term Equine Guided Education in 1999 and co-founded EGEA (Equine Guided Education Association). Ariana's Equine Guided Education Certification Program is endorsed by EGEA.

Equine Guided Education (EGE) encourages growth and learning through the 'Eyes of the Horse'. EGE integrates equine activities, kinesthetic learning and cognitive insight in developing self-responsibility, a healthy self-image, as well as social and relationship skills. EGE can be found in a wide variety of human learning methods including psychotherapy, coaching, holistic health practices, general education, youth at risk and rehabilitation programs.

Horses are an ancient archetypal symbol in the human psyche. They represent dignity, honor, beauty, strength, power and endurance. For thousands of years training one's horse was about creating a partnership of balance and oneness. Less than a hundred years ago horses were our vehicles of transportation, agricultural support, physical laborers, and warfare partners.

Yesterday we took great pride in training our horses for show and sport. Today horses are our teachers and healers helping us reconnect to what has heart and meaning in our lives and assisting us in re-aligning our mind, body and spirit so that we can walk into our future with grace and integrity.

EGE stands for the respectful integration of horses into human learning methods. We see that the horse does more than assist or facilitate learning, the horse actually "Guides"-(One who can find paths through unknown or unexplored territory) the process of "Education"-(Cultivation of mind and character through study or instruction).

Equine Guided Education can take a variety of forms and specialization once the practitioner has become certified as an Equine Guided Educator. Some examples are leadership, self-discovery, self-esteem training, youth development, parenting, team building, self-awareness and rehabilitation.

Ariana Strozzi and SkyHorse Ranch faculty offer a unique, somatic approach to the certification program in Equine Guided Education. We know that it is not enough to just focus intellectually on human learning and development. To develop self-awareness and choice requires working with the mind/body/spirit of the person, the whole self.

45597921R00129

Made in the USA
Charleston, SC
28 August 2015